Stake

Stake

POEMS 1972–1992

Alfred Corn

COUNTERPOINT
Washington, D.C.

Library of Congress Cataloging-in-Publication Data
Corn, Alfred, 1943 –
       Stake : poems, 1972 – 1992 / by Alfred Corn.
              p.   cm.
       Includes index.
       ISBN 1-58243-024-1 (alk. paper)
       I. Title.
       PS3553.0655S72   1999
       811'.54 — dc 21   99 – 16302
                                                               CIP

Jacket, text design and composition by Wesley B. Tanner / Passim Editions

Printed in the United States of America on acid-free paper
that meets the American National Standards Institute
Z39-48 Standard. ∞

COUNTERPOINT
P.O. Box 65793
Washington, D.C. 20035-5793

Counterpoint is a member of the Perseus Books Group

10 9 8 7 6 5 4 3 2 1

First Printing

Contents

From *The West Door* (1988)

From *Autobiographies* (1992)

Stake

Branch or sapling honed to a point and lodged in earth
to say, Here is where we live.
Maypole at the center of a circle dance.
Tent peg driven in the wilderness of exile.
Claim entered on newly opened territory.
Grub advanced to the miner in hopes of a return.
The anchor to help conscience keep its commitments.
Defense of Jael and of the peasant who has no armory.

What is your stake in this?
If existence is a lottery or a game,
then it is played for the highest of all —
and no mistake.

Foreword

T.S. Eliot's assertion that his books were really all one poem impressed me as I was publishing my own, whether or not I could live up to it. But poems sometimes gain from cutting, and, when that's true, it usually takes a time lapse of several years before the author can distinguish between the essential and nonessential. The comparison is too strong, but making a selection can feel like deciding which children you can dispense with. Even the gawky or misbehaving offspring is dear to its parent; this process hasn't been easy.

In the instance of the long sequence "A Call in the Midst of the Crowd," what I dropped was a series of prose documents interspersed between the poems, all having to do with the geography, history and people of New York City. These sometimes directly introduced a poem; for example, just before "Some New Ruins" came a *New York Times* article describing the bombing of Fraunces Tavern by a Puerto Rican nationalist group — the building one of New York City's oldest and the site of Washington's farewell to his troops at the end of the American Revolution. In the same way, the poem "By Firelight. *Die Winterreise*. Death of Henry Hudson" gains if the reader recognizes the title of Schubert's song cycle and is aware (as the prose segue explained) that Henry Hudson was abandoned in an open boat in Hudson Bay by his mutineering crew several years after his explorations of what would become New York harbor.

When I addressed myself to this volume's other long poems — the book-length *Notes from a Child of Paradise* and (nearly as long) "1992," it was the body of the sequences themselves that had to be excerpted. Readers interested in seeing the complete picture have the recourse of looking up the original books or to clamor for a reprinting; the perplexed surgeon will welcome either of those alternatives.

The current selection is not a "complete poems," then. It does not include *Present* (1997), which my publisher Jack Shoemaker at Counterpoint has kept in print, and, in any case, I suggest that no one should regard it as a marble slab laid over the late lamented author. In fact, a new volume is on its way, with luck, the inaugural in a series of many more. Given that early volumes had gone out of print, it was time to make an early recension of what I've done so far. The captain extending his nautical welcome at the top of the gangplank usually includes a formulaic word of caution to arriving guests, and this page has been my equivalent.

Alfred Corn
New York, July 4, 1999

For Grace Schulman

FROM

All Roads at Once

1976

Promised Land Valley, June '73

The lake at nightfall is less a lake,
but more, with reflection added, so
this giant inkblot lies on its side,
a bristling zone of black pine and fir
at the dark fold of the revealed world.

Interpret this fallen symmetry,
scan this water and these water lights,
and follow a golden scribble toward
the lantern, the guessed boat, the voices
that skip across sky to where we stand.

You are vanishing and so am I
as everything surrenders color,
falling silent to vision. Darkness
rises to drown out the sky and silence
names us to the asking boat.

Who echoes who in the black mirror?
Riddles are answers here at the edge.
And still, we can imagine some clear call,
a spoken brilliance blazing the trail . . .
ourselves moving out across the sky.

Chinese Porcelains at the Metropolitan

It was as though I had stumbled
On an unrecognized need, this
Rich embarrassment. . . . For once, I really looked,
Pressing the glass that defended them,
My native state, my own feelings — from what
    Source — caught up in and congruent

To the bulge and flow of those forms,
    Splendid in unimaginable
Glazes: *clair-de-lune, mirror-black, tea-dust,*
Celadon, ox-blood, famille noire, peach-bloom,
Imperial yellow, café-au-lait,
    Fish-roe crackle, and *blue-and-white.*

This last one was its own country —
    Silken pillars of milk dribbled
With a blue syrup that slid down those hard
White slopes, improbably assuming real
Shapes: a branch, ravaged with plum blossoms,
    A house, man, or frightened dragon.

Then, *famille noire:* I was confused
    At finding myself a moment
In someone else's dream, as a drooping
Peony explodes; spring through sunglasses,
Onyx skies, the threat of a striped wing. That
    Was plenty. I retreated to

An unfigured vase of clear green:
Near-real pear or ideal teardrop,
It seemed to lean up against weight, solid
Impetus, recording the smooth action
Of the potter's wheel that hidden still whirred
In the risen gyre of the form.

Form and color, ancient, modern
Captors, saying a shape in clay
Can trace the curve of largest concerns, brim
And not overflow with a full version
Of self. . . . I read the supple script of those
Lines, poems across the trenches

Of time: *You've met the past and it is*
Present. The struggle has not ended,
Will not end. Meaning is only a moment
Contained; but form is legion. The rainbow lists
Go on as new invasions spin up from dream.
Everything still remains to be done.

Dreambooks

Out of the unreal shadows of the night comes back the real life that
we had known. We have to resume it where we had left off and there
steals over us a terrible sense of the necessity for the continuance of
energy in the same wearisome round of stereotyped habits, or a wild
longing, it may be, that our eyelids might open some morning upon a
world that had been re-fashioned anew in the darkness for our pleas-
ure, a world in which things would have fresh shapes and colours, and
be changed, or have other secrets. . . .

— *Oscar Wilde*

A cold night held the clandestine —
After eight o'clock all books were banned.
Under cover, transfixed, I read
And memorized fables by flashlight.
Dream-confections shone in that pale
Epergne of light — tidbit, chestnut,
Nosegay, marzipan *fantaisie.*
Daytime misfits, the balls (flame-stitched).
The bats (oak) that always withered
In my hands, convicted as frauds,
Left me to my bed companions
(None as sticky as the Hardy boys):
Andersen, Grimm, Lewis Carroll.

Perfect programs for tone epics
By Mahler, pure nightmare fodder —
Limbs severed in the Black Forest;
Caesarenwahnsinn of the Red Queen;
The fishwife who tried to be Ms. God;
The Match Girl, burning and freezing;
The six enchanted Swan Brothers . . .

A flock of possible illusions.
Bluffest comforter against cold,
Each story exploded in brief
Artificial fire, then vanished,
Resuming limbo — until next
Reading.
          Now for the sandstar-spill:
Clumsy duckling clasps all his matches
In a fist, loneliness-, hunger-, cold-
Defying, urchin's inkling of death.
Images ignite a blue gas-ring,
Aster-halo, Paradise headgear.

Not Paradise or Limbo. Hades,
A theater of rounds and riddles.
Dreambook, opened to read the future, where
A painful few will have the courage
Of their imagination and live
By it. Reared on absurdities,
To whom the usual was ludicrous,
I naturally accept the first
Person of the Dream: *Snow Queen, dragged up*
From the Frozen Lake of Betrayal.
Brittle specter, scattering eye-splinters
Of diamond, an icon in ermine,
Lace, and pearls. . . . Those glass eyes know me —
From some old hex party probably.
What should be my hand is extended
As — surprise — an aigrette. But of course,
I'm the sixth son, bird imperfectly
Sleeved in a shirt of nettles; part swan,
With an artless limb, flight-worthy, if laming
And useless for swordplay — or base hits.
In my chest I feel a lump of ice.

Grim fairy tale. "Once upons" are always
Puns, double understandings for
The double life, to be read and dreamed
Until the secret order appears.

Night turned the page: dawn would reveal
A figure like a frozen bird
Buried in drifts of wool. Burnt out,
Its battery dead, the flash lay
To one side. A mirror opposing,
All too lucid, reflected gray
Squares of light. Morning announced its
Fictions, a steeplechase laid out
Straight, as on a chessboard, instincts
Reversed in glass. Off with that wing!
Another day's prose to get through.

An Oregon Journal

I

Afternoon: the waves are pure change when the tide
turns, and the defeated eye pulls back
to drop anchor in rock. Deserted by water,
the cliff base was a drying seascape of
green anemones and steel-blue mussel shoals
crackling in the painful flood of air.
Then the predators, marigold and liver-pink
stars fallen in dancers' poses in rock pools,
flattened against barnacle crusts.
                                        You are
there now, made large by time, observing;
the expansive hair stirs, relaxes.
You picked up an empty mussel shell, still twinned,
and offered me half, old tarnished spoon,
the thumb-sized hollow pearled in gray rainbows.
Something in your looks or the thinning light
says we won't always be together.
Back there, topheavy clusters of white
everlastings tap against the sea breeze.
I don't think you saw them, or me, testing
the bone-hard blade of the shell. I tried
to break it, then threw it back to the great
factory of ocean where it will be
ground up and recast as kelp, fish, bird,
star — or another instance of itself.

II

                          The temperatures
appeared, then a snow-blue delirium,

possibly the source of the first images:
to step out at night on to audible sands,
mind brooming aside hazes above
the tossing surfaces, to feel fever against
the silhouettes of rocks.
                              A milk moon,
no, a broken aspirin changing leaden mist
into platinum with its sour light.
                                    We saw
the reflection of a salty star in the wet,
this side the reach of the waves. . . .
Not recollected in tranquillity;
as if we could ever rest and the waves
not echo in our inner ear, high tides
not come forward in feeling change. The best
themes are the moving ones, those closest
following the skating hand that records,
balance, the motive of figure and line.
      My eyes dilated, I tugged the threads
of daydream texts as each day passed
and our night clock, moon-dial, grew fat
with the time we spent.

III

Morning and a garden path: leaves looking
edible as lettuce except for their saw-
toothed margins that promised bitter green juice.
Hydrangeas, huge indigo sponges,
the fleshy petals sopping with dew.
Flushes of lavender — one deliquescent
bloom, bending drunkenly on its stem,
bopped my shoulder as I passed, a morning
shower. . . .

I said, during our walk
to the woods above the sea, "Only two things
make life worth the trouble —
One is love."
      "The other?"
           "Memory."

It seemed true — how else get past the dead
stretches of time without opening the album
of faded pictures, old fumbles, old dances?
Without the touch and spark of skin, sheets, the dim
fireplaces of half-closed eyes? Always less feverish
than I, you suggested, "Conversation. Art.
Food. Drink." A reasonable summary.
    We climbed an unfamiliar hill, lit
with leaf-filtered silver; practiced naturism,
love, memory. Staring as we moved into
the sun — a huge brass flower opening in my head,
daylight shocked into stillness.
                  I lay back
to take in the changes, resting in
my world, who couldn't know yours. Above,
flimsy poles, topped with tepees of evergreen —
the firs swayed, lightsome, stirred again
quietly in the easy breeze. It was blue
beyond, but the clearest indigo, an essential
ink. So we lay. A hummingbird took
our clothes for flowers in the even green
and brown about us. It flew up with copter
motions; hesitated, perplexed at the cloth,
and left as it came.

IV

At noon: a Japanese salad of brown kelp
crunched underfoot. Up toward the dry,
driftwood, abandoned sculptures, antique
metals deeply scratched according to the grain.
The sand changes right before our eyes,
wide-wale corduroy, dry drapery, cross-
patterns in dull gray moire. Everything is
moment, the colors, the lines. We invent
the world and a wide cup to catch it in:
I saw tough, beautiful sea grass rooted
in thinnest sand, and wanted to say it.
Moving discoveries, fever, sand-flow,
voices demanding form for days
that have forgotten their colors. . . .
It began there, among the changing blues
and scored silver. *I will make something,*
bright lines for mine or someone's use,
light from other worlds breaking on this one.

V

The drive to the interior — other trees.
Landscapes, green surfaces punched through by
country rooftops shingled in satin-gray.
Maples were putting out the first yellow,
and we pass a non-town the signs call
Remote.
            So tiring always to drive downhill!
Myrtles and spruces filed past, unhurried.
I recognized the red-skinned madrone,
a sort of myth-tree, one a child
might have drawn. It seemed out of place

there among the elegant constructions
of spruce and fir. The conifers, so old
they are out of time, stand ever new, blue,
sempiternal Xmas trees.

VI

An inland cemetery:
at the summit of a long, hot hill,
reddish earth and brown oak leaves; a grave
formality of tilting stones dated
in sixties and eighties. "Mr. Daniel —
His Death Made Heaven More Necessary."
We disputed the interpretation of it.
       Not far, under the ragged shade
of a moss-eaten madrone, a rotting stone
choked under a tangle of vetch. Some
bleached plastic flowers starved in the sandy ground,
chartreuse and pink. I guessed the true complexion
of death, almost laughed, and then I heard
the rattle of locusts in the heated weeds. Were they
poisonous snakes? I was glad to feel fear
again — no thanks to death, who makes living
almost unnecessary.
                    We each looked
for monuments with our names. You found one.
Thoughts were locusts as I sat and watched them,
pinpoints darting among the indifferent trees.
When we left, the stones were sorry we couldn't stay.

VII

Stopping in a hotel, arbitrary room
of closure. Everything finds margin

in shaded zones — sea, love, time past.
The journal could serve as anchor,
fixity of fact in the great blur. It was
this way, except for omissions, concessions
to tact, daydream, form; and the singling out
of persistent detail, changes, electric
blues and silvers — the way you later find
a thread in a texture that seemed nothing
but puzzles and tangles.

                         Will I ever stay
in that room again? The proofs of the past
are still washing in, manuscript crowded
with change, curly with deletions. Someone
pauses, resting a hand on the silver
knob, trying to remember precisely.
But instinct, deferring to a final
revision, waits and leaves the door ajar.
The ocean says the past is a project
To be continued.

The Documentary on Brazil

For David Kalstone

This window frames an alien climate,
Fern-border of frostwork arranged
Around my reflection, whose faint tan
Winter light dilutes to transparence.
The snowscape out there looks drowsy, what
With those temperatures, night coming on;
And doesn't notice the thundertones
At my back, the loud television
Blizzarding indifferently. I hear
But don't see its Brazilian Eden,
Choosing instead my black-and-white still:
Lessons in geometry, scattered
Houses, rapt trees mere line drawings
Of themselves. . . .

                Photograph and movie —
The real's unlifelike, and snow never
Figured in Adam's coolest dreams. Still
Acquired tastes are strongest, and sages
May see it as fortunate, this fall
Into an unfriendly habitat.
Curiosity and stubbornness
Laid down the fireplace, wove this wool — or
Civilization, its discontents.
We thought ourselves into winter then,
And now thought is most often the frozen
Lace that screens us from the major drawbacks
Of the enterprise. Thought and art,
The pure blind seasons.

Not much light left,
And scrim has hardened into mirror,
In which a thousand pewter orchids,
Soot-black toucans, fluorescent monkeys,
Develop ever sharper contrast
In the glimmering tube-window just
To the left of my ear. Light splinters
Among the ice-fronds, shivering off
In every direction from the bright
Collision of three disparate worlds.
Which subsumes which, it's hard to resolve.
The eye adjusts to those darkened panes,
Preferring a mirror to the rest:
Self's the long exile we appear to choose.

The Bridge, Palm Sunday, 1973

It avails not, time nor place — distance avails not. . .
— Whitman, "Crossing Brooklyn Ferry"

The bridge was a huge sentence diagram,
You and I the compound subject, moving
Toward the verb. We stopped, breathing
Balloonfuls of air; and noonday sun sent down
A hard spray of light. Sensing an occasion,
I put my arm on your shoulder, my friend
And brother. Words, today, took the form of actions.

The object of the pilgrimage, 110 Columbia Heights,
Where Hart Crane once lived, no longer existed,
We learned, torn down, the physical address gone.
A second possible tribute was to read his *Proem*
There on the Promenade in sight of the theme.
That line moved you about the bedlamite whose shirt
Balloons as he drops into the river, much like
Crane's death, though he wasn't a "bedlamite";
A dreamer, maybe who called on Whitman and clasped
His present hand, as if to build a bridge across time. . . .

We hadn't imagined happenstance would lead us next
To join with the daydreamers lined up before
An Easter diorama of duck eggs, hatching
Behind plate glass. The intended sentiment featured
Feathered skeletons racked with spasms of pecking
Against resistant shell, struggling out of dim
Solitary into incandescence and gravity, and quaking
With the shock of sound and sight as though existence
Were a nervous disease. All newborns receive the same
Sentence — birth, death, equivalent triumphs.

Two deaf-mutes walked back the same but inverse way,
Fatigue making strangers of us and the afternoon
Hurt, like sunburn. Overexposure is a constant
Risk of sensation and of company. I wondered
Why we were together — is friendship imaginary?
And does imagination obscure or reveal its subject?
The ties always feel strange, strung along happenstance,
Following no diagram, incomplete, a bridge of suspense. . . .

Sometimes completed things revisited still resonate.
I'm thinking about Crane's poem of the Bridge,
Grand enough to inspire disbelief and to suspend it.
The truth may lie in imagining a connection
With him or with you; with anyone able to overlook
Distance, shrug off time, on the right occasion. . . .

If I called him a brother — help me with this, Hart —
Who climbed toward light and sensation until the sky
Broke open to reveal an acute, perfect convergence
Before letting him fall back into error and mortality,
Would we be joined with him and the voyagers before him?
Would a new sentence be pronounced, a living connection
Between island and island, for a second, be made?

Pages from a Voyage

I

Friends tell me in partly concealed shock
To "build myself up" — by which I gauge
Distances come, the skull pushing out
On its voyage through flesh. All the work
Of elusive viruses during the dark
Two months of this year. Stowaways,
Saboteurs, the worst of them have jumped ship,
Leaving me to convalesce, kill time
With reading (from Darwin's *Voyage*), thinking.
Strange, considering that thought itself may be
A disease when one decides perversely
And with a familiar sinking sensation
To get to the bottom of everything. . . .
Don't ask me what my motive was.

What would Darwin have answered?
Adventure? Knowledge? A journal entry
From Cape Verde, his first port: "The scene,
As beheld through the hazy atmosphere
Of this climate, is of great interest;
If, indeed, a person, fresh from the sea,
And who has just walked, for the first time,
In a grove of cocoa-nut trees, can be a judge
Of anything but his own happiness."
An auspicious beginning; also shore leave
Was a holiday from his perpetual
Seasickness; from bad food, close quarters.
Maybe he should have asked that fair island
Moment to stay: he will return to England
An invalid, imaginary, or perhaps really suffering

Undiagnosed from Chagas's disease.
What am I suffering from?
A fevered imagination, to begin with.
Waiting for health is a painful game
Of patience or like painting by numbers:
Art as patient therapy, but not always
With therapeutic results. I drink tea
And honey; look around my place and see
Repairs are needed; but don't do them.
When the holidays from fever come,
I go out, do errands, charm back normality;
That is, try to recognize it.

But the city, the air, the crowds,
Tone-rows of car horns caught in traffic —
Cacophony? Music? This is the world
We inherited from him. I'm adrift,
Guilty of dereliction. A mendicant
I scan each face as it passes,
If this one might offer some response,
Feeling, intelligence. (A mistake
To try such an experiment in this city,
I know that.) Mostly one sees
Vanity, interest, in the bad sense;
Sometimes lust in action, unwelcome now.
Or vacuity: faces, eyes, shallow saucers
Any lukewarm broth can be poured into
And held for a while. It seems
Everyone asks to be deceived.

Some of the women at least seem comfortable —
These hardy young mothers in pants and canvas
Shoes, guiding the unruly strollers just ahead;
Comparing notes on childhood and the big

Questions: Sex, Age, Health, the Phases.
Almost unconscious, they've lost interest
In appearance; wear no make-up; cut
Their own hair, shorter than men's.
Who are these goddesses and what is
The immense power behind the carriages?
Hard to believe any human she, fully
Comprehending the grade and length of pushing
One of those babies all the way to adulthood,
Wouldn't run screaming into the night. . . .
But they get through, one day at a time.
Childless, I can only guess at that day.

Finally one is reduced to life,
The conditions of life: what matters?
Where am I deceived?
Irresistible gravity of truth
Drawing us forward, deeper into the future,
Whatever the conclusions.
The Darwin who returns after five years
Holds title to the name of a stranger
Who began the voyage. . . .

The Ages of Man are always beginning,
Everything reshuffled, yes, and just when
Youthful optimism, gone senile, retires
From active duty. Each age a maiden
Voyage; and who still feels eligible?
I live days of strange complexion;
Thought stumbles on many moods and words
Come in curious ways, the language
Of discovery and emergency.

For diversion, I see paintings:

II   *Mortefontaine*
                — J.-B.-C. Corot

Feather-grey, and bending left of true,
A tree rises from the heart of matter,
Shade for water, recreation, dreams.
The place is speckled with lacquered leaves,
Light-flecks scattered casual as grain.

Sun infuses the general cloud,
The lake a pearled cloud also enjoined
To symmetry in which the temple
Twins, improbable here — as the boatman
Mooring a shallop behind the birch

Is not. Unaware of him she does
Needlework. Outdoors? But the painting belongs
To fiction, not truth. . . . It's puzzling, the charm
Of an ideal that does not reflect
The bare, actual life at hand.

He perfected the world; but I resist
And will not see symmetry if none is
There. The charm's broken, diversion spoiled.
His mirror shows my own reverses. Life
Is breath: the world clouds over, gray with loss.

III   *A Separation*

The errand that brought me here is clear enough,
But what made me turn just now, eyes filling
With the sunset over the blue park, the hidden river?
Trees of no leaf; half light assumed to be sun,
A pale yellow with silhouettes of branches.

Come back unspoken bends upward with suppliant limbs —
Addressed to memory. This was our turf. One of these streets
Led us down to the park as often as weather allowed;
Even when it didn't. For example, there was that rainy spring
Toward the end, your mother off on the *Beagle* tour
Of the Galapagos, the forecast here so discouraging;
My hand nonetheless dabbled in the stream of a passing
Hedge. . . . We stopped to acknowledge rainwashed irises
That fleurdelised a bed along the way.

One of these comes back as emblem for all —
A hum, a blue daze, no actual color;
And a suspicion of lemon creeping out
From the throat, spreading over a tongue
Printed with ramified blue.
We always admired the same things. . . .
No, not always. Memory grimaces, goes sour.
In fact, we often disagreed. You weren't prepared
For a symbolist's habits of mind, I imagine.

Beauty's inadequacy to the world: a proposition
Dismissed or countered by careful selection,
Crossing the fine and fragile with the plain and hardy. . . .
Even at this moment the vestigial aesthetic eye fastens
On what might be a huge petal, veined with branches
And hanging from the iris of midwinter sky; I could see it
As an emblem, the blue and gold complex of what we were.
But the emblem doesn't quite do the job, I know that.

Enough. What would have been seen at one time fails to satisfy
me now. Once I might have used lateness and my errand to sug-
gest the flight of time and the doomed quest for an always more
distant past. Experience arranged in a splendid contraption. . . .
But no. It's literally late and I do have an errand, not related to

the past. To tell the truth, I can only guess who we were; it's been too long. What's most present now is the suspicion that beautiful emblems are a kind of lotus-eating, myths that mask the truth. (I feel agreement rush in from all sides.) And yet, avoiding the gorgeous, adopting the plain and hardy, do we finally get the truth? I wonder if that might not just give us one more mask, another myth. . . . It's not in this frame of mind poems are written, and, indeed, there's no poem here. These are only midwinter thoughts, another effort to come to terms with us; or with terms themselves, which, I suppose, should be means and not ends.

IV   *To a Friend, from a Landing*

The hours spent here accumulate like building blocks
Exactly the cube of your black-walled living room.
Consideration increased in a repeated setting:
Glass and chrome, flowers, ice, white sofa, clay elephant.
Often there was music or reading. The good life, no?
I reviewed each print suspended on your invisible walls;
Difficulty wasn't part of the picture, apparently.

You're at your post in the rocker; everything should be
Normal. But conversation lumbers, elephant-like, weighted
With memory. (When was it you gave me the Moorehead book
On Darwin? You thought I'd like the toucan pictures.)
Consider the ruins of the afternoons — spilled ashes,
Chaos among crumbling towers of books and albums.
Surface disorder: but surfaces are often profound.

We're both subdued, reduced; both changing, we say.
Still, there's tea, whole-wheat toast, honey —
Amenities. We nibble and sip; and I ask how
The yoghurt-maker's doing. And is Spenser
Really good? Deliberate questions, deliberate answers.
Caught in the comedy of change, it's as though each

Spoken word is meant to stay mutability, its terrors.
We struggle to compose some device of sincerity —
A device, two-dimensional, emblazoned on armor,
But distinguishing friend from foe. We struggle,
And, frankly, we'd like to go back to small talk.

But you have never been so present before:
A whole room funneled into moving gray eyes.
I put down the cup, not knowing whether to go or stay.
I'm thinking about the life of friendship, good and bad,
A mixture of pleasure, misreadings, shared jokes,
And the blind, inept desire to be shield and ally,
Equal to the changes time accumulates in us. . . .
I can't find a device to say this, not yet.
At a turning point, covered with confusion, I make
My escape; but reluctant to go. I'm on the landing;
We shout and laugh, cheerful, friendly, stranded.

V

Collecting its virulent specimens,
Could the expedition go too far?
Think of Darwin feeding the Benchuga bug
With his own blood and contracting himself
To a lifelong disease — all for knowledge.
Belief torpedoed; and history
Hasn't recovered yet. Not that a credo
Drawn from the mortal body is beyond hope;
Just that time is short, the poison spreading.

After 1859 Europe makes steadily
Toward materialism: Darwin, then Nietzsche,
'Social Darwinism,' *laissez-faire*, Fascism,
Ethology, Man the Hunter and Killer.

Darwin's little finches quickly evolve
Into chimeras all with a common ancestry
Of good intentions. Case in point:
The eloquent enemy of slavery
Becomes a source book of racism.

Good intentions; and still the scientist
Is fascinated by murderous nature:
"One day, at Bahia, my attention was drawn
By observing many spiders, cockroaches,
And other insects, and some lizards, rushing
In the greatest agitation across a bare piece of ground.
A little way behind, every stalk and leaf
Was blackened by a small ant. The swarm
Having crossed the bare space, divided itself,
And descended an old wall. By this means
Many insects were fairly enclosed; and the efforts
Which the poor little creatures made
To extricate themselves from such a death
Were wonderful."

VI

We move toward our opposite;
Opposite except for a thin film,
A membrane of experience. Biography,
Like history, repeats itself, a pendulum,
Or like tacking zigzags into the wind,
The saw-blade of a risky expedition,
Version plotted by dead reckoning:
The ship moves out to the edge of the world.

For Darwin, several sightings of death —
Encounters with Indians, rounding the Horn;

Or the earthquake at Concepción:
"A bad earthquake at once destroys
Our oldest associations: the earth,
The very emblem of solidity, has moved
Beneath our feet like a thin crust
Over a fluid; — one second of time
Has created in the mind a strange idea
Of insecurity, which hours of reflection
Would not have produced."

This season only accelerated a process
Always under way; as though fever
Fired the boiler of some
Auxiliary engine — forward
With all speed until the block cracks.
It was a premonition of shipwreck.

After days dimmed with fever,
And two nights brilliant with sleeplessness,

It began to pound, loud
As a throttle, a mechanical thing.

All night, again no sleep. By morning,
Complete, jerky exhaustion.

Stumbling on sea legs to the bathroom mirror:
A gauntness, bones cased in waxy flesh.

Dull, dead eyes, no feeling.
I felt a kind of abstract compassion:

No one should have to go through this,
No human being . . . which came

Only because of the certainty
That it could not be me,

This dead face. Otherwise
Pride, refusing to pity

Would have interfered; an absurd
Scruple at that moment.

No one should have to — but they do, and worse.
Eventually a pill dragged me under.

VII   *A Foretaste*

Down to the water, in no hurry.
Stood and looked across.
Neither tempted or untempted. ·
A landscape reduced to signature.
Waited and watched. Considered
The last water and the useless sky.
Then turned and came back.
I remember this dream in characters.

There's a special queer radiance now —
Notice an open milk carton, or lettuce
Drying in the colander; a ray of light
Crossing the floor in afternoon.
Also, a mistrust of things:
The colors are paler, experience
Frangible, like weathering limestone.
It's all ready to collapse into chalky ruin.

VIII

The Galapagos, Melville's *Encantadas* —
Carapaces of bubbled rock and black sand,
"Glowing hot"; they supported lichen, cactus.
Here evolving suspicions hardened into certainty.
It anticipates our own reptilian landscape.

The tortoises: man-tall necks, mournful faces,
Every day a transport. They take their trailers
To the waterholes and tank up a month's quota.
Mating comes as a collision of armored cars.
Barring crack-ups and slaughter, they are immortal.

Or the lizards: cold-blooded half-smiles
Swaddled in slack leather. Harmless.
But nonplussed by these curious observers.
Darwin grabs the tail of a burrower:
"At this it was greatly astonished,
And soon shuffled up to see what was the matter;
And then stared me in the face, as much
As to say, 'What made you pull my tail?'"

Reading this paragraph, I can see its genial author.
I hesitate; I clasp the hand of a friend.
That, and the rest, force me to will his book,
And along with it, the consequences;
According to the practices of friendship
Among scattered witnesses across date and place;
Introductions arranged by books;
The true heritage, where descent
Is called tradition, culture
A sea of competing species:
Only the fittest survive,
But those for all generations.

Lines inscribed in blood,
Chromosomes of word
Coupled at the crossing
Of tradition, mutation,
Generate a book —

Form fit to the purpose,
Source reborn as a new
Origin, living afterwards,
Mating with kindred minds;
Breed true, sole offspring of mine.

IX

The future attracts with the help of ignorance.
It's hard to believe he would have made the voyage
If he had known the consequences. Still, it would
Have been a shame to miss the Andes, their fossil
Shells; the bland, unearthly bromeliads;
Ostrich dumplings; the coconut-eating crab;
The flamingos and their hieroglyphic reflections
At sunset waterholes; the tattooed Maoris. . . .

Summing up the value for future voyagers:
"In a moral point of view, the effect ought to be,
To teach him good-humoured patience, freedom
From selfishness, the habit of acting for himself,
And of making the best of every occurrence."
Maybe so. I've made the best of it I could;
And this morning I find myself saying
As my sum that the point is to realize we do
What we do — to have it 'happen,' beautiful
Or terrible. It seems that the choice between bliss
And knowledge is no choice at all,
Not for the species of Adam.

Sickness and health coexist unjustified,
Become a part of each other.
There's something electric about life —
One feels protective of its ignorant optimism.
The body, like a child, doesn't know
About meaninglessness or death;
It's ready for dinner or a kiss.

Things always begin. There is
A pile of fresh-stamped letters to mail;
The back of a neck to squeeze;
Nails to be hammered with well-judged strokes;
A shirt fallen on the floor in an expressive
Attitude; and the way a ribbon of poured honey
Folds backward and forward on itself. . . .
So many minds to become, events that might be
Beheld, the heart of matter through which a conditional
World springs colored, solid; seizes there.

I'm feeling pressure now
From the suspect messianic;
But intentions here were mostly good,
And the record at least recognizable.

I feel — alive. There's been a reprieve, this
Surprised minding of the glad sense in things. . . .
Everything is still moving, and it's possible
To consider other voyages over the rim,
Incautiously curious about the animals,
The unclassified flowers of the future.
This round goes to me.

On the Beach

In this dark
will we know each other
the North Star
changes its mind

And strands of cloud
go with the drift
of prevailing currents
no answer comes forward

It may be the tide
will turn bringing
the barest outline
a remembered form

Enduring a world of water
I keep dreams company   waiting
for the stars to wheel in place
as image   story   future

A Call in the Midst of the Crowd

1978

Darkening Hotel Room

I

The glass on the picture from the Bible
Has gone pale and reflective, the mirror dull.
A room of rectangles, dark door moldings,

Gray windows; mind itself turning corners
From sleep to awareness to attention
To notions. Up and down the hallway doors

Open to boom shut. And always less light.
The porcelain lamp exists only in silver
Outline, drawn something like those solemn curls

On the pillar capital silhouetted
Outside. Ninety winters this room has housed
Other selves — young women in long dresses,

Men like walruses bearded. Bibles, crochet,
Ointment. They would be gathering for warmth
Around the fireplace that now stands empty,

Dark, cold. Others fell asleep in this hour,
That ornate pillar the last image formed
In closing eyes, the curtain descending.

II

Something between dream and not-dream that goes
Back thirty years and a thousand miles
Away: I almost see her standing

At the sink, wearing . . . a cotton blouse, slacks;
A little thin, what with rationing,
A husband in the Pacific, three children.
She glances at the turk's-caps and lantana
Outside — no, that was a later house.

Afternoon light models her face into
Fatigue, kindness, a worry wrinkle
Between dark brows. Curly hair,
Short and not well arranged. In another
Room someone misses a note of the scale;
And she bends down to me, a mound
Of not much more than self. She smiles,
Her head turning this way, that way. . . .

This is possible, but of course not
Real; unless every picture held in
Thought silently is real. An uncommon radiance
Attaches itself, like the candle's,
To the strain and flicker of recall,
Small incandescence, halo at night.
It appears as a gift, second sight
With the power to transport in safe conduct
To lost houses, forbidden rooms,
To when she still — . But it can't be
Memory. I remember nothing. Absence.

Which came grotesquely, with toys
And birthday cake, they told me later.
To reach in confidence for efficient,
Bony arms and only find — .
Puzzling; and it still is, how
A bereavement, immaterially, goes on,
An asceticism, for a lifetime.

As you might choose caution, and, what,
Thoughtfulness — in order to survive.
Survive! The blunt desire to endure,
Imagining what might be restored.
I don't remember, nonetheless see
Light, afternoon, as she bends down
In large outline, like a cloud approaching.

III

The man wrapped in darkness is free to dream:
All those I invite may inform this space,
My company until the darkened room
Rises to the surface — coming back like
Someone's biography, summoned up whole,
To be relived and almost understood.

The bearded man may have done as much —
Suddenly reaching out for the young woman
Banked next to him in the loose braid of sleep.
At night's lowest point he divides and numbers
His consolations. She stirs, yawns, neither
Understanding nor minding his rough hug.

But I won't wake you. Sleep, love, rooms that
Shelter us, for how long? The speed of night,
Of thought. Older than my grandparents . . .
Worlds later, gray light restores a picture
Of the Master teaching his disciples,
Indifferent to, unaware of us.

The Three Times

The first will no doubt begin with morning's
Stainless-steel manners and possibilities
Out of number. Sunlight scold too much?
So a tense gets thinned out with solvents,
Preternaturally bright with the will
To swap laziness or pleasure for paper money.
The future may appear as a winter day, colors
Of the façades like frozen jellies and sherbets,
Palaces of frost in crystalline order;
Then fall into shards at the approach of fact,
A needle of starlight aimed at your heart.

This one has all the force and danger of
Randomness: image drips into daydream
As waters gather to sea level and go
With the tide. Clouds. Chain lightning.
The waves move in like destroyers. And —
And only subside when, for example,
I stop to prove a cup off-center
In its saucer. A door closes, footsteps;
The night outside warm and silent
As an underground parking lot; askew stacks
Of books and papers; raw material;
Clues to a life. Because it's the time
Of pain — always the same — and pleasures:
Taste, touch, work, walking, music — not one
Of these trivial and all incomplete.

The last was always a famous storehouse;
Or you sit down before an amphitheater
Of tiered keyboards, repertory of stops;

To choose diapason, bourdon, vox humana —
A stone wall, the shadow of a leaf,
The gate I saw and then the grass
Running in place before the wind.
The place of the mind moved on, just
Failing to be everywhere at once;
And reconstructed an autumn afternoon
From the highest window, when the buildings
Forcing up against an imposed sky,
Fused into background, embraced the park,
Rested. The last baseball players
Swarmed around a tiny diamond template;
Man and his games a perfected miniature —
Like the past you almost don't believe in.
Yet it's there, behind perhaps a blue veil;
Sturdy; calm; unless put out of countenance
By drab standards of exactitude.
The last word was never, was always
About to be written; so that none of us
Could know whether hope, become action,
Exposed to the elements — a bronze monument,
Negligible among the surrounding towers,
But somehow truly central — would corrode,
Crumble, dissolve; or weather into
A fact of nature, continue to be.

The Adversary

I

In cold spring, a bird of passage, species
You don't recognize, precedes you, just as
The hills retreat into dusk or fog, blurring
Toward the last color. What I might have said —
But the heart's gone out of it, so that
Late footprints only fill with mud, blunted
Purpose. Removed in the house of your thoughts
You hear nothing. A word falls from parted lips
Revealed in the dim light as almost half
A world; though you by force of being everywhere
Never appear. Who believes he follows his own
Intentions, if all of them end with you? Again
The city raises its trophies among the clouds,
A final myth. Nothing left but the desire
To speak the truth. This is yours, the silver
Cord is severed, and the case reopens.

II

You survive, you have accommodated
The miracle, and nothing was transfigured.
Your mind, the cold day, the hills
Flatten to scenery, just as expected.
For only to appearances are you wise.
You see them as a given, disorders
Mankind is heir to, clinically named, each
An oasis, possibly mirage, marking
A listless horizon. Old harmonies, reconciled
Nature, accuse one's errors of spirit.

You hesitate over the next step, a habit
Contagious as cold, the subject forced
To keep mentally indoors, light off the snow
Discovering each outline, multiplying
Possibility until — until your mood changes.
Would you know me in some other guise,
Still mirror, you there, intending no
Special malice, who, neat and impartial,
Blight what you touch? The drama did not unfold
In a temple, your premises drab and general,
Contact a dumb show, the stratagems
Of performance and policy, coming and going.
I wanted to take life to my lips like
The simple water — and your hand intervenes.

III

Surely I've seen you before, the candid
Eyes, poised head marbled by thought as air
By smoke? And *you* called them, family
Of dreams that descend in slippers
The carpeted stair, fatal company, one
After one? You withhold what you know, as
Substance begins to rub away, mist from glass.
If this were repose, no complaint; but
Something stings, an inevitable drop
Of acid in the solution. The cold hills
Wait for us, spring's coming on strong.
Nothing left but the desire to speak the truth,
Drawn by the power that lies in discredit.
Where are you going? You look pale, the glare
Goes up in volume, drowning you out. I am
To understand: Nothing human is alien to you;
And so you are mortal. The black tunnel roars
And suddenly opens out into space

From A Call In The Midst Of The Crowd

Poem in Four Parts on New York City

JANUARY

Night swallows up everything but doesn't
Alone cast the shadow inside, this sense
Of incompleteness, lack
Of echo. . . . I expect
Too much? Too little? My undetailed season
Only appears in the bright particulars
Of paired headlights flooding an avenue,
You'd say, at cross-purposes with Number.
If the worst certainties were skill — but now
Down comes to out, and words crumble, refuse
To sign their names, empty noises rattling
A barrenness their failure parallels.
People, like a people, do have slumps, when
Nothing wants to be said, and what is,
Hardly worth anyone's staying awake for:
A satire for unaccommodated men.

Best, they claim, to remount the horse that threw
You (in the present case, a horse with wings),
An act demonstrating,
Proving that you are — what?
I've forgotten. Reach, grasp; moth, star; and
"He's the very wishbone he breaks in two."
How to sustain it, the doubtful subject
Of a self in neither sense exemplary?
In those doorways a man will freeze tonight,
Disappointment's victim, failure at love,
Dazed, benumbed — hardly more than expression.

Sheer perversity, I guess, makes me plumb
The mirror of this self-imposed city for
What, if anything here, holds a promise,
The speaking gift that falls to one who hears
A word shine through the white noise of the world.

Midnight Walk, St. Marks Place

Biography repeats itself. Couples break
Apart. This could be that same winter spent
Just down the street, a short walk from the grave
Of Peter Stuyvesant; our divorce pending,
Cheerless tippling, useless midnight phone calls,
The commonplaces of pain — which makes us
Anybody. Now, chance brings me here again:
The buildings in dead Auden's neighborhood
Discovering their age,
The cornices revealed
As snow eyebrows over extinct windows.
Snow underfoot; and notice how snow not
Muffles but makes a miniature of sound,
The tiny scrape of a shovel on concrete,
The barest hush as my breathing out turns
Into frost. Walking alone, one hears things.

Times like now, a life moves forward one foot
Before the other and by discipline
Alone — Auden's practice year after year,
You can tell. A willed punctuality.
Look, I've come as far as
The Astor Colonnades,
Mansions let fall into ruin, along with
Any number of encumbering passions. . . .
Now snow falls down in fistfuls, clabbering

The slopes of cars into anonymity —
A transport to simpler times, that pale gold
Window lit not electrically; and here
A blue spruce thrown out after Epiphany.
But those tinsel icicles, windblown sidewise,
Are strictly post-World War, like me. And times
Are simpler now, really. Just what's wrong with them.

Nine to Five

The first days of the new year go on trial,
Destinies sluggishly reassumed
As handed down, the summons delivered
By the thrilling of predawn alarms. . . .
Radios follow you down the stairwell,
Sound from apartments like rival perfumes —
Symphonies, pop tunes, talk shows and weather.
A day surprised by rain, which falls down viscous,
Almost snow. Your umbrella snags on awnings
Or locks horns with others', and there a broken
One lies like Dracula dead on the sidewalk,
Silk heart pierced by a silver
Ferrule. No one comments
Though chatter precedes you, enters, and fills
An elevator as doors close with steely
Conviction. Now the several perfumes

Blend, no, clash like rival radios. . . . And
Will the sentence of connecting rooms ever
Be understood, the dull fluorescent glare,
Standard desks, floors and machines, routine
Greetings and drab coffee, the undertone
Of sex and violence? Backstabbing and lust
As antidotes to boredom:

Kill time; but don't seem to.
From your window tarpaper rooftops blacken
And silver under a grainy fallout
Of gusting sleet. There is no sun, there
Never has been. Personnel across the street
Just like you, clock-watchers all . . . The last hour
You see that snow, with colder resolve,
Blown into dense emulsion, has printed
A halftone photograph of January.

Tokyo West

Eating out alone, one makes solitude
More remarkable. Better this, I suppose,
Than the day I've spent trying to feel actual
In the absence of a human echo. . . .
I sense a counterpart in the waitress,
In fact, each recognizes each from last year;
Sleeker, less urban then, less desperate,
Maybe, but the same person, one who has
Clearly been suffering the strain of exile.
Hypocrites both, we smile.
"Clear soup and sashimi."
Too bad the décor happens to include fish:
Goldf— calico, really; that don't mind being
On display and gambol like kittens in
The bright tank. Hooked over its edge, a tube
Injects a downward fountain of bubbles

That quickly fall back to a ceiling they
Flute. A westerner in barbaric diving
Costume surveys this world through the grilled
Eye of his helmet. Everybody looks
At everybody. And I wonder what

Detail of my appearance so rivets
His attention, that Japanese, whose hair,
Sheared down to teddy-bear fur, rivets my own.
Enough that I'm alone,
No doubt, or don't look away
Fast enough. Oh, here's the soup — clear as mud.
"I'm sorry, didn't you say bean?" "Never
Mind, I'll have this." So few things ever come
Clear anyway. For example, tonight
At my place I've left on the FM, *mf;*
With no one to hear, is there music or not?

What to make of things? Walking home in fog
And cold, full of beans, raw fish, tea, rubbing
Shoulders with so many of us, exiles
And at home — the fat girl in jeans and leather,
The black policeman, the streetwalkers with
High boots, hopes, and Pompadour hair — I feel
The misery that loves company; which may be
A worldwide motive for swarming in cities.
Assemblage of the homeless, on the move,
Apartment, job, lover, self, everything
Improvised, raw, temporary; and I
Discover how strange it is to work all day
Then dine — no, eat — alone,
Like so many others.
Anonymous, at loose ends, finally
I belong. They swim forward to greet me.

By Firelight. Die Winterreise. *Death of Henry Hudson*

Three heats sting us almost back from numbness:
A skin-tightening fire; glass globes of brandy;
Traumatic dream song in German, which scalds
Like liquid wax from windblown candles, fear

And pity spilling in streams of semitones
Down the staff. For as long as a stylus moves
In in inward spirals, until it stops,
Whatever stillnesses, colds and darks that
Prefigure an end, when by favor of night
The city departs from life, entombing them
In turn, its masters, its captives — for who
Finally controls? — all
This may be put aside.
In fire, fed by my hand, a catalogue goes,
Enameled pictures of what I do not want,
Page after page, curling into crepe; and

Scarcely warms, though with each flash the trembling
People of flame, in spiritous blue, unfurl
Another dawn and another farewell.
You are here; it does no good.
Abandoned to the fogs
And dims of self, Hudson set hopelessly free,
Adrift among the floes of candle ice,
Mountains of gray wave, the vast overhead
Where delirious prophecies play like flames:
Lost dreams of Passage, infernal machine,
A fortress of towers in which the damned
Follow ever-lower spirals to a final
Trough that slowly fills and packs them down in snow.
The coldest of them, crystallized as he is,
Still remembers a former life when two
Drank at a fire, silenced by separate dreams.

Some New Ruins

Certainly a revolution hardens.
That it should become a museum piece,
Like this tavern, troubles. If this new war

Succeeded, then the ruins would have to be
Rededicated; put on display; then bombed
Again. The dust never settles, finally.
Brokers quoting prices over lunch here,
Heirs of the Founders, forgot their history.
Securities — illusions; yes, and so
Is security under a régime
Where death may be served as the consommé.
Would they have given up wealth — that is power —
If they'd known life depended on it? But
They must have known; and still
It made no difference.
Our births choose us; then our lives; then our deaths.

The past is what has to be exploded,
A message everywhere outstanding. And
Our immediate interest in survivors,
In centenarians, somehow becomes foolish
If awakened by surviving currents
Of feeling, centenary architecture,
Whatever has escaped the empire
Of the new. Guilt by association:
History's suspect right from the start
For having calmly housed injustice, constraint.
Here's what they chose to bomb:
Bricks laid in Flemish bond,
White trim, windows that *open;* ship-tight build
Of a dwelling drawn on a human scale.
One hellish machine deserves another?
Steel boxes stand all around untouched.

I can't pretend to go along with it.
Death eludes restoration; and the killing
Keeps coming back as the recurrent fact

About them, overshadowing the rest.
An eye for an eye: the future darkens, goes blind.
I I I I — sounds like hammers, building
A barricade of rage. With just causes they
Rush into guilt as toward the state of grace.
It's not really the sadness of ruins
I feel, but rather the fact of mangled
Bodies; bloody rags; something smeared on the walls.
(This is too hot to handle, can't be done,
Or done well. And will make no difference.)
True — though arbitrary and
Abstract; just like justice.
The ambiguities speak for themselves.

Earth: Stone, Brick, Metal

It has the shape of
A boat with the Battery
For prow — and was always in overhaul
As the thresholds and lofts rose and fell,
Then rose higher, harder, until they became
As inevitable as landscape. Now
Embedded in brute stone, a man struggles
To emerge. He does all you do, in greater
Volume; has an anatomy that functions
Much like yours, but for all soul only what
An occasional rare observer lends,
Citizen or outsider; and if you see
Dawn wreathe the city in a mythic
Light, it may be he has appointed you
For this role. There is no helicopter like
The mind's eye, nor any weather better

Than a clear cold winter

Afternoon, say, to be
Lifted as high as the neutral splendor
Of five hundred high-rises that with frank
Hauteur cleave the North American air.
From the sublime expanse of the bridges
Alone one could die. Human and daily
Tributary pours in from the boroughs,
Dredged up by trains that with sudden magic are
Airborne, over water, afire with cold
Sunlight — before they funnel back into earth.
It rumbles underfoot, a resonance
Of granite, metals, ice. From the gratings
Plumes of steam rise to annihilation
Above the glassy branches of a bare tree
Tossing in the wind's manage; and through these,

A glint of distant steel.
You are carried forward,
Log in the rapids, jammed at a spillback;
A bus swims from curbside with one sad rider;
Limousines deposit precious cargo
At the Four Seasons; tricolor flags turn
As barber poles over the Museum,
Fountains drained, air sharpened with a stench
Of charcoal and sauerkraut. Sausage-linked coal-scows
Nose down the Hudson, afloat the blinding
Waters of sunset. Laundry flaps in the slums;
And just before dark, the windows ignite; now,
Lamps in bright strings cross the park. The skyline
Is jeweled; cold; like nothing else on earth.
Like nothing else on earth the restless hum
Of this place — a question not yet answered.

APRIL

Awakened before I meant
By soft shocks outside, white wet
Light streaming in at eight or so.
That I carry my daze intact
To the window, where at a remove
Unfocused patches of color float —
Taxis, trucks, early risers —
Things that move and beep and talk,
Each on its comic errand, proves
This a day set apart. But how so?
White petals fallen on the floor.
Time to throw out the dogwood branch.
Think of all the flowers that suffered
And died for me, not deserving it.

Bits of the dream come back:
The Elysian Fields. Yes. Which looked
Like a boulevard, not a meadow.
Theaters. Cafés. Great has-beens
In the fancy dress strained out
From three thousand years of Western Civ.
Silent they stood in poses grave.
It seemed a certain stiffness
Was de rigueur among the dead;
Or they distrusted a body
Who hadn't yet arrived.
"Ages since any of us lived;
Not done now, flesh so outmoded,
Inelegant, opaque." Togaed
In vapor, a gray mirage at last
Spoke four oracular commands:
Travel. Love. Suffer. Work.
"You mean experience, knowledge?"

Know no more than you can do. Though
Knowledge is power, absolute knowledge . . .
The rest was lost under drum rolls,
A procession headed toward the arch
And flame votive to the Unknown.

Good speechmaking; but, as advice,
It's superfluous, no more than
What I've always done by instinct.
In time you come to balance the more
With the less remote. And compose
A life out of to you plausible
Nouns and verbs; convincing others
As well. Today will make a kind
Of pure, arbitrary sense, then —
Like that blurred array of colored
Patches down there, conjugating
In bright steam, rapidly changing
As thoughts, plans, thoughts about plans.
Occurs to me the city is
A print-out of habit; and small wonder
I belong here with difficulty,
Restless, feverish with those four
Imperatives, navigating
With few instruments, my own
Method none but a mad desire
That everything be near at hand
In a world's monumental fluidity.

Even now five years drop aside
Like scattered documents: the day
Of the solar eclipse, and I
The last through a gate of the park
Where others wait quietly.

At the vacant top of a low
Rise I settle myself on dead
Brown grass for the viewing. The air
Goes yellow-gray, a color western,
Say, twenty years ago. Silence. Little
Breezy cyclones. The day reduced
To poor facsimile. Three figures
Below, aiming a pinholed card
To spotlight crescents on paper —
Something like a burning glass,
But cool, precise, droll.
All of them stand motionless,
In contrapposto, elbows crooked,
Casting ghostly shadows on the earth.
A boy gazes up through a shard
Of smoked glass (dangerous, I've heard),
And the river stumbles southward
In unwonted twilight.
The scared stillness doesn't break.
And notice the grass by magic has
Communicated a wet coolness
To the seat of my pants. Then
It's over. The world wakes up.

A trapezoid of light has shrunk
Toward the window. Without moving.
Things dreamed and done and known:
The record is there that others read,
Notations strewn in my wake,
A language of roadside flowers,
Mostly illegible now to me.
The wasted passion stuns, as a cloud
Might pass across the mind's eye,
The dream of life opaque to life.

Water: City Wildlife and Greenery

The most prolific seem to be imports:
English sparrow, Tree of Heaven,
London plane, and now ginkgo, which
Threatens to take over quite a few streets,
Dioecious, the female letting fall
A rank fruit, yellow globes that rot
And make sidewalks slick and hazardous.
Then, urban dandelion, harpoon leaves,
Mustard buttons coming up through pavement
Cracks, along with crabgrass and plantain. . . .
Times I cut Queen Anne's lace in vacant
Lots and brought it home, where it reigned
For a day and then dropped white snow
On the mirror table. Once or
Twice I brought back some sunflowers;
But they drooped and expired by nightfall.
        Pigeons are more or less a weed
Here, though often handsome in mourning
Plumage, gun-metal and black; also,
Café-au-lait, calico, and newsprint, some
Scarved at the neck with liquid green
Rainbows. Then, the squirrels, mostly gray,
Which keep to the parks and freeze at human
Approach — what is it their tails are asking?
Frightened, they ripple over the grass
And embrace their way up a tree, where
At a safe height they pose as broken-
Off branches.
                At the waterfront
Seagulls, each one uniformed in neat,
Nautical whites, glide and levitate,
Looking like a sort of elastic mobile.

The Hudson yields unpalatable eels
And shad that some people fish for and eat.
Of the common animal species, many
Live in the parks: frogs, a few fish,
Earthworms, beetles, chipmunks, snakes.
And nearly every bird of passage
Has been sighted there at least once.
        The pests include huge foraging rats,
A population of roaches always on the point
Of doubling into infinity, any number
Of mice, and in summer, plagues of flies,
Plus a troubling number of mosquitoes.
There's a special problem with strays —
Ribby dogs and cats that run wild
And live out the fate of any creature
Abandoned to the streets — cold, damp,
Hunger, begging, violence, early death.
Spring gives some relief to this sad business.

Two Parks

Sundays the Park-Fast opposite,
Conglomerate-owned, most likely,
Is empty — until a mother, white,
And a father, black, come with their son,
And a yellow ball and a blue bat
For his first lessons. The father
Wears a cloth cap, maroon T-shirt,
Suspenders, and loose denim pants.
He's tall and stands there, arms
Akimbo, pants flapping in the wind.
The mother tightens the belt
Of her cardigan, buttons the jacket
Of the boy's denim suit. They move

Across the asphalt, over parking spaces
Marked in yellow paint. The lines
And numbers seem to play a part
In the game; but don't, in fact.
Batter up: the man throws, the boy swings,
And — strike one. When the ball bounces
Away, he bounces after it, then stops:
Don't Go in the Street. She
Retrieves the ball, then helps her son
Get a good grip. And, when the man
Throws again, the boy, steadied,
Guided by his mother, connects.

Everything seems absolutely
On the surface today, planar,
The world its own gloss; though still,
I suppose, lit by me from within.
Same wind, same sun, but altogether
Different, three days later. The mixed
Blessing of free hours, a mind that wants
Something to grapple with — which need
Not be rare. An outing then, to that
Museum of seasonal change
That lies between the Metropolitan
And Natural History . . .
                                        However,
The mood's wrong, the day, who knows why,
Poorly chosen. Too late now. What to do
When the sense vanishes of . . . self?
This from-the-ground perspective
Offers no clues, nothing more
Than a vast general fatality —
As though gravity pressed down harder
On an outstretched body. To have been

Drawn by the lodestar of an absurd,
Unrealistic project . . . Wouldn't
Anyone have been flattened by it?
The historical dimension alone —
Sheer weight of lived lives,
Massed sufferings, crunch of time
Rolling past, cries of those falling before
Its wheels; vanished triumphs; naïve
Dream of all the dead somehow
To have counted, to have *prevailed.*

The visible facts here by rights
Ought to console: one hundred thousand
Pink cherry blossoms; which, however,
Hang uselessly, of no rescue now.
Time passing, and beneath the tree
A man passes, bearded, with side curls,
In black Orthodox clothes and hat.
Blackness and pinkness go blurred. . . .
Not far away, paired teen-agers, one
Atop the other, lying motionless.
Stunned by light and the new season.
Somewhere children playing war,
Treble savage screams threading
The distance. An idea arcs
Toward me, thrown from the blue:
That, in the long run, life tends
To become a spectator sport.
Is that welcome? On the contrary,
And not to be taken lying down.
More foreground! Zooming in
On pink things, a heavy bumblebee
Bobs, undecided; dangled, it seems,
From a spring everywhere at once.

Putting aside the element
Of fatuity in this, I'm drawn in
A moment by the spinning wheel
Of mere appearances; sunlight;
The all-pervading hum of change;
And how a vast mausoleum, charged
With remains, balances against
An image of blind, of minute,
Indefatigable purpose.

Billie's Blues

Louis tried to negotiate a connection on a bus.

The best we could was a couple of single seats on a crowded bus. It took me back twenty years, to be headed to New York, the way I had so many times before: busted, out on bail, broke from paying the bondsman, hungry from having no time to eat, beat from twenty-four hours without sleep, remembering the smell of that jail as I rattled around in a damn bus with a sleeping sailor falling all over me. But all that I soon forgot, with my man.

— Billie Holiday, Lady Sings the Blues

Their red lamps make a childlike stab
At decadence. Now and again a hoot
That pretends to know too much. And all
Of us jammed tight together in
The clubbiness of drinking. Gauged pressures
Of a hip, an elbow, mean whatever —
Nothing, or the first step toward
A glance, an appraisal, a mirrored
Interest. Also, a mirror reflects
Shiny bottles and the company behind
One's back: studied nonchalance, arched
Or puzzled brows, flight jackets, scratching
Of a beard. Clichés from the juke box

Suddenly ring true; so that I leave
The bar — and none too steady — for
A corner table a mosquito candle
Beacons me to. There. A relief
To have stopped being after anything.
Who needs it? Besides, one cruises
Mainly to cruise, navigating from island
To island, not counting on landfalls —
Though in fact I met you in a place
Much like this. You. So often
I've thought the word in that upper case
We use for what is one of a kind.
Thought, and sometimes written; wondering
Whether dispensing with names,
An apparent gender, showed, oh,
Cowardice, betrayal; or good sense.
I always wrote to You, supposing
The alert would catch on anyway.
And not wanting to seem a special case
Myself — though who isn't one? Holiday,
For example; with her ambiguous first name.
Nothing vague about the voice, certainly.
Listen: love mixed with a little hate for
Him. Sounds universal to me.

Impression

Brightness of the May five o'clocks;
Chatter of the mob at book
Parties; silver from a ringed hand
Holding a glass; and the shiny new
Patent of a foreign shoe . . .
A hush falls over the dilute
Outdoor evening; men in pale

Linen suits. One more naïve sky
Sent up from Bermuda. Monet
At the Modern: *Ces nymphéas,*
Je les veux perpétuer. . . .
The light in this woman's eye
Clear and tart as quinine soda;
Murmurs and laughter as we push
Into the lobby; the ballet
Is blue and black and white and tense.
A day in the mood of New York:
Cool, rounded, undetailed, in soft
Dull colors. The water trembles
At one's step in a glass vase
Of lilacs. Impersonal clouds.
Starched shirt collar scratches slightly.

Spring and Summer

Only three seasons in this city, really.
There's something French about late May,
Early summer. A stroll down the avenue
Next to the park, under alleys of trees
Heavy with the spring water they've drawn up
Into new leafage; and now breezes lift a branch,
Which falls back into place languidly,
The way you imagine a Renoir model moved —
A slow heavy grace. I'm thinking of green
Lattices, white lattices. . . . Notice how
Even the policeman on his scooter, helmeted,
Goggled with mirror glass, looks dreamy,
Sitting there off duty under an elm tree,
In the green air that smells of water,
Earth, and lindens — mint-fresh, like each
Neatly cut, serrated leaf of the beech

Overhead. A girl in a thin flower-print dress
Goes by. Sunlight in a complex pattern
Falls on her face through the openwork
Brim of her straw hat. Now, an old man
In a half-sleeve cotton shirt, striped blue.
His shortish pants reveal large anklebones,
Sheathed in thin lisle socks. Feelings
Sound like chamber music today: flutes,
Oboes, strings, a piano spattering softly
Into the basin of a fountain. . . . Now
A taxi goes by, with bent celluloid reflections
Of buildings and trees flowing across
The windshield. Fluffy flocks of light
Stir on the pavement. Still, a current
Of pain in all this, like a hot stone
Applied to the chest, weighing down
The proceedings marmoreally. If I
Were to die, let it be on a day like this.
Starting now. And by twilight, as people began
To leave the bars, soothed and rounded by one
Or two drinks, to gather at the theaters
In Lincoln Center, or take a last stroll before
The park got dark and dangerous, I'd begin
To feel it slipping through my fingers
Like fine sand, as everything goes dim, the hum
Of traffic, cries, horns, sirens, a couple
Laughing as they step into an elevator;
The sky complex as a bruise; the sound
Of leaves coming through the window as I go out,
Leaving my city and the people behind.

JULY

Fire: The People

Toplight hammered down by shadowless noon,
A palindrome of midnight, retrograde
From last month's solstice in smoke and flame,
In molten glares from chrome or glass. I feel
Fever from the cars I pass, delirium
Trembling out from the radiators.
The dog-day romance seems to be physical,
As young free lances come into their own,
Sunbrowned, imperial in few clothes,
Heat-struck adulthood a subject to youth
And fitful as traffic, the mind pure jumble
But for that secret overriding voice
Advising and persuading at each crossroads;
The struggle toward freedom to forge a day.

Smoke; flame; oiled, gray-brown air.
Jackhammers and first gear on the avenues;
Stuntmen driving taxicabs; patient, blue,
Hippo aggressiveness of a bus, nudging
Aside the sedans. And the peculiar
Fascination of a row of workshops —
The dark interiors with skylight sunstripes;
A figure walking in slow motion among
Pistons; rough justice of a die cutter;
A helmeted diver, wielding acetylene,
Crouched over some work of sunken treasure
That sparkles gold at a probe from his torch. . . .
Seismic shocks interrupt this dream — a stampede
Of transports flat out to make the light,
Mack truck, Diamond Reo, a nameless tanker,

Hi International, a Seatrain destined
For the Port Authority docks — one more
Corrugated block to pile on the rest,
Red, green, gray, and blue, waiting for a ship
In the Grancolombiana line. . . .
The seagoing city radiates invisibly
Over the world, a documentary sublime.

Lunch hour, even the foods are fast, potluck
In the melting pot: the Italian girl
With a carton of chicken; Puerto Rican folding
A pizza; the black woman with an egg roll;
A crop-headed secretary in round,
Metal spectacles eats plain yogurt (she's
Already mantis thin) and devours glamour
Mags. . . . Our crowd scene, a moving fresco:
But is it really there? The adversary
Today is named Random. How capture all this
Without being taken captive in turn,
Install it as something more than backdrop,
As a necessity, not a sundry?
Suppose just an awareness of the way
Living details might be felt as vision
Is vision, full, all there ever was — this
Instant palindromic noon, the joined hands
Of the clock, end and beginning. . . . Surely
The first to consider imagining stars
Constellations had already done as much,
Just by making some brilliant connections;
Mind crowned itself in a round of leaps from point
To point across the empty stage of night. . . .

* * * * *

Now as a pigeon banks, descends, hovers,
And drops on asphalt with back-thrust wings,
Comes a desire to be lifted in the balance,
Rise to some highest point and then be met
By a fierce new light haloing lashes shatter
Into spears of aurora, naked eye become
Prismatic at last and given to see in kind
All the transformed inhabitants forever go
About their errands, on a new scale: the rainbow
Is the emblem for this moment filtering through
The body's meshwork nerves, and a heartbeat impulse
All around puts troops of feet in step with music,
Persistent, availing, that disregards the frayed
Years, vagaries, downfall among trash, accident,
Loss; or because it knows these rushes upward
On something like heartbreak into the only sky,
Air aspirant with fractioned voices, feverfew
Of the sensed illusion, higher ground, progressions
Sounded in the spheres — so each step takes them further,
Sceptered, into daytime, saluting the outcome.
There is a fire that surpasses the known burning,
Its phoenix center a couple that must be there,
Blast furnace, dynamo, engendering a city,
Phosphor spines that bend and meet to weld, to fuse
As a divining rod — sluicings, spillway, braid,
Chorded basses that set myriad threads afire,
Newborn limbs and reach of the proven tendon now
Let go into empowered brilliance, rayed showers,
The garden regained. In this light the place appears:
Hands that rise or fall, muted gestures of welcome
And good-bye, face that turns and comes forward to claim
A smile latent in the afternoon air, vague crowds
Falling down streets without character toward
An offered covenant — love that gives them each a name.

Sunday Mornings in Harlem

Overcast skies I never welcome.
Time changing hands, right to left,
Rushes forward, upward as smoke,
A cataract on the eye of day.
Cloudy Sundays, our morning walks
Ten summers ago, framed now as by
A jagged hole knocked in the scummed pane
Of the present. We walked despite
The strange color of our faces, stares
From those up or still up at that hour. . . .
A strivers' row: bright brass knocker,
Heavyweight in memory; cedars
In concrete urns flanked a stoop;
Brownstone acanthus and palmates
Mind can still conform. Then, hotboxes,
Some of them gutted and refilled
With garbage. Clouds. The fat air
Sweated. Smoke and fumes. Drew us
On into streets of junk, excelsior.
Ruins. Tumbled ashcans, fluted drums
A broomstick hammered. Somewhere sirens
Whined, and the radio did a tap dance.
Ten pigeons rose in an updraft like flying
Newsprint. A heap of burning trash and tires.
The wino, a conjure, suddenly giant
In profile, let fly a rich curse at who
Passed. Smoke of the past; shoots up
Like carbon into suspension if not
Solution and now flows into the veins
Of a drawing, a tattoo it still hurts to touch.

Declaration, July 4

It enters its second hundredth;
The oldest and still somehow
The newest. Restive sense
Of nationality once again
To be appraised. A birthday at least
Is a holiday — hence their picnics
In Riverside Park, where they come
From hopeless neighborhoods
To cook over charcoal, to laugh
And play catch or Frisbee, all
In the shadow of that Tomb James
Unaccountably "liked" and praised
As a symbol of military might.
Steady expressway whiz of cars nearby.
Grownups, those with the means, have
Left us behind in charge today.
We all but believe something untoward
Might happen — not just mischief.
A true celebration; and that,
Oh, for once we might feel
All of us belonged in the same space,
Company, instead of crowding.

In fact, mischief is the more probable.
If only it took an effective form. . . .
Seize the city before They came back?
Then suspend all TV transmission
Until the rest of the country
Came to terms? Just kidding, of course.
Passive, dulled, all hang separately
From the branches of government
Among other negotiable leaves.

It still seems grotesquely
Shortsighted: "I've seen the future,
And it's on unemployment."

The future. Who doubts the tomorrows
Of the world are manufactured here?
Differences disaffirmed dwindle day
By day, on every continent.
Distinctions blurred, satellites launched,
Experiments made — the one under way,
Perhaps not noble, will test whether
Society can subsist by law alone,
Without common purpose or myth. Breathless
Hush as we wait for the outcome. To live
The gamble tastes like gall,
Brings one to the revolting point.
Yet the only character of that
At hand is the written; and most of us
Doubt that the legible legislates.
No fun, playing skeleton at the feast;
And sometime again I'll probably
Even run through that little charade
Of stepping into a voting booth
To pull the crank for candidates
Surveys pronounce already defunct.

Patriotic? In a way. In my own way.
Asked to celebrate the land (though in fact
No one asks), I would begin with a standard
And for me unavoidable gesture
Toward the landscape, my memories of it.
Then, the people, many of them, and their —
Our — peculiar qualities; even though
With each of these goes a corresponding

Fault. (That most Americans are far
Too sincere ever to learn a foreign language
Proves something.) Qualities, achievements: I
Would single out "accessibility
To experience"; and that wild comic sense
Under which anything at all can be said;
Our inventiveness; willingness to let
Convention lapse when it no longer serves;
Impatience with absurdity, pomp,
And bombast; sticking up for underdogs;
That thread of quietism and plainness
Introduced by certain dissenting settlers,
A formal seriousness surviving here
And there in some people, objects, houses.
I would celebrate the hybrid music
That grew up here, made by the untrained;
And those soft coastal cities — Charleston,
Savannah, New Orleans, San Francisco;
And if not his cons, then Jefferson's prose
And his house; the eccentric, forceful works
Of fine art made here, and the movies
Of the thirties and forties; I would praise
The cosmopolitan receptiveness of this city,
Its countless allusions to an entire world.
And I would celebrate, if I could, the language —
English new-alloyed in the melting pot,
A tool enabling who can use it to build
A city like this one, where superb Beaux-Arts
Temples and libraries stand cheek by jowl with
The native clapboard, International Style,
White Castles, cast-iron, urban high-rise
Vernacular, Prairie School, pizza parlor,
And Greek Revival. For language here is
Federal, eclectic, ad hoc, laissez-faire.

Others will seek substitutes for "nifty,"
"Glitzy," "dumbbell," "drag," "pizzaz," and "cool,"
But I won't. Freedom of speech! For, like all
Dreams, the American, if it prevails,
Will prevail in language; or just vanish.

Also, now that the sun bids fair to set
On our Empire, the picnic done, a world
May be free at last from the American War.
Surely that calls for celebration?
Let all pyrotechnics that can be mustered
Begin: epithets explode in sharp reports,
A long tirade in the grand manner rise
Into heaven like a Roman candle,
Hyperbole on target with bursts of
Brilliance clauses depend from, dying falls
Generous as sundews or thistledowns
That seed the waters with artifact fire;
Then rise again in periods that never flag then do,
Blue night a field for star-spangled banter,
Where red and white verbs shoot lightninglike down,
The air all abrupt with an echo of the old
Oratorical thunder: "We hold these truths
To be self-evident; that all men. . . ."

City Island, Pelham Bay Park

We keep meaning to visit Pelham Manor
But always end up here instead, among
Dried reeds and beer cans, sunbathers, same old
Fishermen; and rowing crews out on the blue
Expanse, "their force contrary to their face" —
Spenser's figure describing the progress
Of June; July he sees as naked, astride

A lion. No lions in sight, but plenty
Of almost naked people. I find myself
Wanting some spiritual analogue;
And say to you I wish some day I could
Put down in words everything passing through
My mind now: alarm over how we all live
Or fail to — dinners out, theaters, sex,
Drink, gossip, Valium and Librium, vertigo . . .
And how it all blends in with this day, here,
The dried reeds, the rusting cans, anglers . . .
You're not sure I'm making sense, and besides,
"We are not a Muse." People do the best
They can, you remind me. Agreed. "And yet —
I can't get past the feeling that, almost,
We take a kind of pride in sliding down
That greased track; a proof of sincerity,
Or something like it. *Normal? Sensible?*
Better off — though that's just what we're fighting.
Long as we're 'young and foolish' we're safe;
Half of that at least we can guarantee,
Fling caution to the winds, ourselves into
The next fiasco — fey, charming, maudit.
An overstatement, yes, and by saying 'we'
I get away with murder. Still. I wish
We knew some other way. You sure you *like*
Living up to it all? Up to the minute?
I'm not . . . Well, enough. Walk to the beach?"

*

Bare bodies. "Didn't know sun could undress
So many." Smearing all of its members
With baby oil, a Latin family
Flopped in the shade of a striped umbrella.

Radios tuned to different baseball games.
Vendors yelling the sale of pretzels, beer,
And lemon ices. We spread our blanket on sand,
Among discarded pop-tops. Won't stay long.
The burning attraction even of near-
Nudity palls after a while. People
Become what becomes them; eventually
Fate puts our clothes back on. "Oh, by the way,
Aren't we ever going to try and see
Pelham Manor? I have a feeling not."
Something in my voice makes you turn toward me.
Your sunglasses reflect twin umbrellas,
Red and white pinwheels where your eyes should be.
We stare. We wonder why we came back here again.

Summer Vertigo

Twilight ushered in still so late
By the madwoman, barefoot, asking
Anyone for a cigarette.

It is a street of figures
Mostly dressed in white — no one
You know. Or why, when the large dark
Car brakes beside you, a voluminous
Globe of hair, a woman, should
Turn and beam a smile your way,
Cool waves of jazz spilling over
The dash — before that space drives on.

There is simplicity just
In a streetlight and a little joke
In the bottle that rolls aside
From your step. Too many voices,

Too many echoes. Are looking to be
Amused; have forgotten other
Evenings lost in the same search;
Are general and lack subjectivity.

Willfulness takes you underground:
A labyrinth filled with victims, dressed
In several secondhand myths.
To barrel through darkness at 2 or 3 G's,
Venom coursing through the third rail
And poured into the flywheel at a screeeeching
Halt: you do the stations and take the cross-
Town shuttle to Grand Central — nothing.
Then, head of a man, body of a bull.
Cold sweat beads the chrome fixtures
Of a virginal urinal. . . .
Back on the tracks. Through asperities
To Astor Place, then to the Bleecker Street
Stop: reborn to the world.

Still the perpetual cruise of cars,
Solitude broken on the wheel of Cadillac
Or Ford. Now, follow a gray form
For a half-dozen blocks, in the rhythm
Of your planless plan; so the night deepens
In a spurious threading of streets,
Though you know your behavior
For thin and strange by the blanket
Disdain of all their stares. The remembered
Ideal of being young and footloose
Comes up and shakes its head:
Bottom-lit mask as a lighter grates,
Flares into life and then dies. . . .

Paisaje de la multitud que vomita —
So much to contemplate,
Head drooping downward, amazed
At how stars billionize in the pavement.
A crack in the concrete
Propels you on to link it up
With an old and fatal dawn.
Ah, there's the madwoman again,
Slumped against the wall, feet
Still bare, and taking a rest
So far denied to you.

Birthday Lunch, August 14

"Some birthdays seem to say more than others."
He listens; waits for the development.
"Just try to brush aside connotations
Of the thirty-third year. Besides, the day
Always loomed large for me; because it was
On my second, V-J Day, actually — "

"When you lost your mother. You told me."

Silence. A dream mushrooms over our heads.
Some birthdays seem to say — I feel the date
Is someone joined to me, speaking, my twin:
Halfway along the road of life Brother
In the middle of a glaring city
Tower by harbor and beacon by bell
For us maybe for everyone birth death
Are joined confused this   morning didn't we
Smile and rage together last of the lather
Washed away to see age there like a wince
Permanently installed   separation

Would be the end of us   married for life
Faithful I follow you into a future
Of ifs our constant backward stare ignores
In reckless service to an extinguished life
We scull reverse toward what we disregard
The golden age is past and a lesser
Time persists the wake widening first white
Then dull then blue   morning gives nothing
But a déjà vu the same light falls on
The unwinding script and you feel yourself
A comet moving out toward aphelion
Zero dark and void where no one is son
Or mother no nor anything at all

"Feel a sense of urgency or crisis?
Maybe. Not just because of the date.
This breakup, for one thing. Seems like, like a —
No, a birthday's just a fact, nothing more.
Risk of flying too high on fancy wings.
A comet, say, if it stays numerical,
Can orbit forever. But let it lose
A sense of proportion, become irregular and
Begin to dream of some brilliant gesture;
Then it gets hauled in on gravity's line,
Swan-song flameout in the diamond air. . . .
Fact is the remedy for bright ideas."
He asks where the striking image came from.
"Oh, out of the blue. Haven't you ever
Noticed how the most trivial and painful
Thoughts play catch? Or how, if we could read them,
Those around us might speak volumes. We tend
To take the smiling cover at face value."
"Facts or not, I see birthdays make you thoughtful."

"Mm, you probably mean long-winded.
It's true I have moods — often mistaken
For morals or philosophy. Granted
They recur. Just as their opposites do,
Periodically. Do you follow me?"

"Contradiction is what makes things happen?"

"Or not happen. Or just be temporary.
Us, for example. It's over. And still,
There's always the chance we might patch things up,
Isn't there? Isn't there? Guess not. Not as
They were. Sorry, I didn't mean to — "

*

Much later my double drops in again
For a visit, asks me how my day went.
And if you need me call don't wait until
Next year   nights are tough   TV leaves you cold
I know   be careful   let appetite be
The guide now more than thinking or willing
Flashy gestures of the will to be will
End in confusion and self-destruction
Exalted as a form of vital pride
Or honesty exerts a pull on you I
Who better than I can tell   ignore it
You chose to communicate and so forfeited
The option of not continuing to be
Dialogue   begin that now   look outside
See what there is   a city a text
For you to compose and revise   stay close
To the facts you see   there was that moment
Last month when the people and the place were

Just themselves but more   bring that back to life
Some time the future will have contained
Your past   wait and see   among those towers
You may raise up your own even a tower
Of loss   does that ring a bell   as bell
Or beacon losing has become almost
A lighthouse for us now after ages wasted on
Winning   in perspective is our peace light
By tolling tells us where destruction lies
And shows by shining life is still awake

Bike Ride

I brake to talk to M. — on top of his van, installing a skylight in the roof. His straw cap has its own skylight, a green plastic insert in the bill. Green smiles: "Going out to Colorado for a few weeks. You staying here?"

"I'll be out on Long Island the month of September. Really need to get away." We will, we say, see each other in the fall.

Condemned, closed to traffic, the West Side Highway has no other riders or joggers today. Weeds grow in the pavement cracks. New York crumbles. MAYOR ANNOUNCES DEFAULT. And if the city collapses, the whole country? And if the country? Possible?

A Sanitation Department incinerator. Conduits dump processed slag into a bin. Smoking, dusty excrement, drawn from every corner of the city and reduced to a common brown denominator. The democracy of waste.

Suppose they just let it slide? A brick wall floats past me, long green vines lashing up and around a window, like passementerie. Just imagine how things will be fifty years after the evacuation. All the buildings smothered in vines; first, a merely apparent erosion of form, cornices, pillars, dissolved under a scaly green cover; two hundred years later, an eerie Chinese landscape of crumbling cliffs lost in leaves and mist. . . .

Battery Park. Castle Clinton restored as a fort for the Bicentennial. Too much of history is military. Why wasn't this restored as Castle Garden, to remind us Jenny Lind could subjugate an entire city, just by singing? Or even as the immigration depot it became later?

Again, military history: a dozen slabs of granite listing all the World War II dead. Arranged in double ranks; with a prospect of Miss Liberty. At the end, a huge bronze eagle clutching a laurel wreath in fierce talons. Aggression, sex, excrement . . . But here comes the ferry. Looks like a big, professional harmonica — and gives a long toot as it begins to swing around in a crater of water. The sun's a red ball; water, blue, with red highlights.

Where did that hour go? Back on the highway. A few last assistants glimpsed through the lower windows of the financial district office buildings. Saving the city or bankrupting it? The big clock across the water says it's late. Time to go back; things to do before I leave town . . . Then, from Governor's Island, a trembling bugle sounds taps. Breath catches. Thoughts of New York during the War. Khaki uniforms. "Skirts." Images from half-memories, from movies or half-remembered movies, swim up. My eyes swim. Why is that. Look, a full moon — greenish, august, fat. Saying good-bye. End of summer.

OCTOBER

Another Year

Driving west on the L.I.E., somewhere in
Outer Queens I pass that trumped-up shot:
A million gravestones, ominously super-
Imposed on a gray, one-substanced Manhattan.
Closer in to the facts, the skyline graph
Shows highs around Wall Street, then dips, then soars,
And drops way down around 110th. . . .
Now, as I cross over from Williamsburg,
A sharpened vista: in the tragic sunset
Each building's half gold, half violet;
Art Deco-inspired chrome-plate towers poise
Motionless in the maritime air and stand
As emblems for that urbane high distilled
In the Jazz Age — one Crash made legendary.
The price of this moment: that it's passing.

Bang! The familiar shock of a downtown street,
Civilization and its discounts, all
Foreground. Either you must look up or just
Abide with what's flatly there opposite.
But how the MOBIL Pegasus images
The gift of wings to words like Then and Now. . . .
Coming back always relives the first time.
Ten falls ago; see me there alone, reading
Some novel in the West End Café, dressed
In black turtleneck, gold-rimmed spectacles,
And French-existential cigarettes. Staggered
By my late New Yorker status. It was
Like a new faith, the litany running
Central Park West, Midtown, Village — New York!

And the whole awful following winter,
Left to my own vices, *Nobody* cared.

Vast anonymity, at home again.
Free once more to stroll where I'm drawn, hero
Of my own story — as they are of theirs,
Who could have been me, sitting around scarred
Wood tables in recycled clothes, trading bull
About records, this season On and Off
Broadway, their "real prospects for breakthrough
Next month," what's unique about Balanchine,
Where you can get a good egg cream, well-cut
Bluejeans, or laid. If it's true New York fits
The twenty-to-forty age group best, then
I have close to a decade left to burn here —
Admittedly not with the twenties' hard,
Gin-like flame, Ecstasy? A swelling like
Confidence in my chest. Last year's confusion
And failure, at last, to be solved, repaired!

Orlando Furioso: *Sicilian Puppet Theater*

A painted flat as houselights dim becomes
North Africa. Palm trees. Moorish loggia.
The Saracen king, turbaned, with forkèd
Beard, reviews his captains, each helmet plumed
Black or white like smoke puffed up from a brain
Burning for revenge. A lengthy speech on
Why Christians are bad. One of the hotheads
Swears, with Eastern selflessness, to die
For Allah and King. A loud thwack of the sword
Against his heart: he means business. (Which isn't
Meant in this little theater tonight.
A dozen or so have pulled themselves away

From more underwritten times to witness
A stagecraft relic. When the old man dies,
The show dies, certainty he must ignore.)
But here comes Orlando, Christendom, a fight!

They fly at each other in a golden crash
Of armor — cuirass, helmet, shield and greaves,
Caroming Dodg'em cars, brass on brass, with
High gestures of valor that leave the dead,
Mostly paynim, heaped up like stacks of lumber.
The winners lumber off, appealingly
Proud; and their clamorous miracle shows
How dolls not four feet tall can be larger
Than life. Orlando, moved by his Maker,
Bodies forth legend in part to reveal
Powers higher than ourselves make us brave.
Do puppets return the master that same cue?
Give him a piece of their older action?
If certainty brings all legends to an end,
A knight is whoever still asks questions?
Orlando, sword aloft, speak: what happens next?

Fifty-Seventh Street and Fifth

Hard-edged buildings; cloudless blue enamel;
Lapidary hours — and that numerous woman,
Put-together, in many a smashing
Suit or dress is somehow what it's, well,
All about. A city designed by *Halston:*
Clean lines, tans, grays, expense; no sentiment.
Off the mirrored boxes the afternoon
Glare fires an instant in her sunglasses
And reflects some of the armored ambition
Controlling deed here; plus the byword

That "only the best really counts." Awful
And awe-inspiring. How hard the task,
Keeping up to the mark: opinions, output,
Presentation — strong on every front. So?
Life is strife, the city says, a theory
That tastes of iron and demands assent.

A big lump of iron that's been magnetized.
All the faces I see are — Believers,
Pilgrims immigrated from fifty states
To discover, to surrender, themselves.
Success. Money. Fame. Insular dreams all,
Begotten of the dream of Manhattan, island
Of the possessed. When a man's tired of New York,
He's tired of life? Or just of possession?
A whirlpool animates the terrific
Streets, violence of our praise, blockbuster
Miracles down every vista, scored by
Accords and discords intrinsic to this air.
Concerted mind performs as the genius
Of place: competition, a trust in facts
And expense. Who loves or works here assumes,
For better or worse, the ground rules. A fate.

Photographs of Old New York

They stare back into an increate future,
Dead stars, burning still. Air how choked with soot
One breathed then, the smudged grays and blacks impressed
In circles around East European eyes,
Top hats, a brougham, the laundry that hung
Like crowds of ghosts over common courtyards.
Dignity still knew how to thrust its hand
Into a waistcoat, bread plaited into shapes

How to dress a window, light under the El
Fall as negative to cast-iron shadows.
Assemble Liberty plate by plate — so
This giant dismembered arm still emerges
From folds of bronze and floats over the heads
Of bearded workmen riveted in place
By an explosion of magnesium they've learned
To endure. Then, Union. Rally. March. Strike.

And still the wretched refugees swarming
Out from Ellis Island, the glittering door,
To prosper or perish. Or both . . . The men
Don't see the women; or see how deftly hems
Can be lifted at curbs — well, any eye would
Be caught by that tilt of hat, profile, bearing.
Others strive to have mattered too, stolid
Forms that blush and crouch over sewing machines,
Haunt the libraries, speak on platforms.
Did they? And did this woman, who clearly still
Speaks no English, her head scarf, say, Russian?
A son stands at her side, crop-haired, in clumpy
Shoes. She stares straight forward, reserved, aware,
Embattled. The deep-set eyes say something
About the emptiness of most wishes; and
About her hopes. She knows the odds are poor.

Or, the odds are zero, counted from here.
The past survives its population
And is unkind. Triumph no more than failure
In the longest run ever fails to fail.
Is that the argument against shuffling,
Dealing, and reshuffling these photographs?
They are not mementos of death alone,
But of life lived variously, avatars

Energy, insight, cruelty took — and love.
Variousness: the great kaleidoscope
Of time, its snowflake pictures, form after
Form, collapsing into the future, hours,
Days, seasons, generations that rise up
And fall like leaves, each one a hand inscribed
With the fragile calligraphy of selfhood;
The human fate given a human face.

Afternoon

Scudding clouds give happenstance to the walls
Of the dome above me. Add the motion
Of my last ride this season — cyclist in all
But winter — add breezes, and what a fluid
Day is rushing by. Though the bike always
Takes me for the same ride, for staying the same,
It changes all the more — not a place but
An event, demolition wrought with speed,
As in our downtown urban renewal.
Whereas the Hudson's a static shimmer;
And seagrasses, reclaiming the landfill,
Still wave as they waved by New Amsterdam,
Fond farewells to the poor stone houses of men,
So jerry-built, so variable, compared
To forms in straw that know how to recur,
And so, last. . . . A helicopter lifts off,

A moment signifies. The wheels randomly
Spin after an impulse and gravitate
Down street names I like: Coenties Slip, Pearl,
Broad, and Water. There: renewal can mean
Repair. Fraunces Tavern has been restored
Like new again, or, rather, old. (Still, I'd

Hesitate to have lunch there.) Renewal:
"Dear Love — We've both changed. On a different
And better basis, we'll be able to . . ."
St. Paul's bell strikes five and struck the same tone
For the nineteenth century. But I am left
With my text, no less coherent than its day.
Good citizen, discontent as any,
One who has seen home base as enemy
And ally; and lived in contradiction,
The order of this place, in this moment.

The city thinks, but whose thoughts? Wire service,
Museum, financial directorate,
Creator, conscience — mind's the very air
We breathe. Thought by a place, am I that place?
A part of the whole and the whole in part?
These inspired breezes, once-in-a-lifetime clouds,
Pearl-white autumnal light creating suns
Like whirligigs on the water. . . . My bike,
My charger turns toward home. Towers rise
And swell as I come closer, the pedals
I pedal like a pump that pumps them up —
As such, I am the builder. Though what proof
But in saying it, an act, much like love,
That enjoins substance on what comes and goes?
Streets, stay with me. Desire, match with a moment;
See, that there always be one of this day.

Short Story: A Covenant

Together again under the same roof —
Your car's — and we're driving over to Brooklyn.
When patter lulls, I try the radio:
Haydn's *The Seasons;* and, as it happens,

"Autumn." (*Belt Parkway, Flatbush Ave . . .*) Today
Prosiness feels right; so I don't pay much mind
To the unfolding Verrazano Narrows
And its huge bridge. We hit the approach, lift
Off and begin to cruise. The sun tries to set,
Snagged by arch and cable. We're flying over
Water, Haydn crescendos — well, in fact
It's — in spite of myself an impression
Gets foisted off on me. . . . Then, Staten Island,
Which comes as a pleasant anticlimax.
"There's a park. Want to get out a minute?"
We stop. Just as "Winter" is beginning.

Grass. Fallen leaves. Not much to look at.
Thinking about leaves and about my book —
I'm to have the first copy in a few weeks.
"But that's already — past." I explain; you nod.
We reach a bluff that looks out toward the bridge,
The light begins to go, and as we stand there
I ask: "Think we'll manage better this time?"
You say you can't say. We shouldn't predict.
What will be . . . "Oh, look at that!" A wall of fog
Moves up the Narrows. Wind rises. We gape,
And — it's so fast! — the bridge is overtaken,
Completely erased by a featureless
Gray foolhardy gulls as well vanish into.
Fog rolls up around us. We feel chilled, blank.
And nervously dismiss the obvious
Omen. "Aren't you getting cold? Let's go back."

For the return, I suggest, who knows why,
The ferry. First, a leisurely drive past
Sunday-evening streets — Hope Avenue, Prospect,
Sand, Wave, and Victory. There's the ferry.

They flag us into the hold of the *Joseph*
F. Merrell. Which is painted bright orange —
The inside of a pumpkin. "By the way,"
(We're climbing stairs), "what about Thanksgiving?"
You don't know, no special plans. Whatever.
Doors swing wide, we step out on deck. Nothing,
Just water and gray fog. The blank wall. "Cold?
Take my jacket." You don't; but you think
You'll go inside. I want for some reason
To stay out here. Even though there's nothing
To see — well, those disappointed children,
Who wasted their dime on the view-finder.

Wasting time, wasting time. Are we? I'm afraid.
What new bond could hold if the old one broke?
Fog, tell me what *you* think. Nothing, of course,
Or just what I think. You are gray, but no
Matter, just an involved form of the void
I tell myself to; and there is plenty
Of room in an empty thing, all decks cleared,
Ready to be stocked with whatever I choose.
That might be objects of purest fancy:
"Wan water, wandering water weltering,"
Music of a Rhine maiden or W.C.;
Hallucination of the highest spheres,
Myself an orrery for the whole system;
Aeolian harp, Hades, Bower of Bliss,
Whatever. No. Instead of these, bare fact.
My own moment, right now. Here's what we have:

Children, parents, couples of every
Persuasion. Old women wearing scarves, alone.
Men forty, necks weighed down with camera.
Little girls in ties that scream and munch popcorn.

A Chinese man wiping his fogged glasses . . .
With passing time to be drafted as a kind
Of Chief Executive, my constituents
All of — all of us. But how to begin?
Those promptings. Listen. And thought doubles back
On itself, as before. . . . Your life changes, then
Your mind. A year, a month from now — what? Suppose
We make one more effort; see if we can.
And if it fails, it fails. Go on from there.
A boy sporting a red bandanna dangles
From a ladder, laughing; crying. And we
All make toward engulfment, doomed; and joyful.

Air: The Spirit

Real but departed, like remembered clouds;
As a face seen in water lives and erodes.
Spring days under the locust I look up
And shade my eyes against the sun, dissolved
In a million parentheses, the idea just
To catch my drift by directing a feature
In the tradition of Lumière & Sons.
First, a fantastic silent — moonwalks, love,
Fans flinging roses at the stars; then,
Sound — long rubbery blats of foghorns dubbed
Over our dialogue. An exchange, as
Spirit, in the city, comes to replace
The yes we owe the country earth and to
The earthly contract. For an urban year
The old calendar has to be altered.
Best and last lie upward: a new garden.

In fall, the guest arrived, invisible but
For a skin of leaves plastered on muscled air;

He settled on his back, a sleeping giant.
Leaded outlines against that arctic light:
A steamship, a locomotive, a roadster —
Transport during our jazzed-up twenties.
A thrill invaded the world, and everyone
Plausibly confused the wine of life with wine.
But they couldn't matter to each other in two
Dimensions. Strings hoist my arm and hand
In semaphore gestures across the gulf.
Plural, countless, sand falls in a silken stream,
The sound unreturning except as wind or rain
Trembling through fictive summer leaves. Good-bye
To that stage of things. A black-edged placard says
The world has become manageable again.

FROM

The Various Light

1980

Moving: New York–New Haven Line

Taut on the leash, at last I have my way:
The train jolts off, just for a split-second
Immobilizing a porter I catch sight of
Through my window, pushing his cart. The platform's
A treadmill or a backward rack; for, his feet
Notwithstanding, he grinds into reverse,
Left behind in underground darkness. . . .
That forward-backward prank gets cruelly played
On every car or truck that races with us
Along the paralleling highway; try
As they might, our motion slowly brakes them,
It sends them backsliding faster and faster
Behind; a feeling I recall from nightmares
(Nightmares, and, to tell the truth, from "real life"
As well). Another stunt of overtaking
(Like my own sharp about-face two months back)
Is the fateful rotation a car makes:
Trunk to grill we see it, a slow, pivotal
Display — practiced, in fact, on every near
Item in the window, especially trees,
Their radially branching form flung into perfect
Umbrella turns (clockwise, because I see them
From the train's left side). Indian file they run
And pirouette together, the closest rank
So much quicker than others farther out,
Which fall behind at a desultory pace.
(This constant shuttle between two points has made
At least some aspects of the pattern clearer.)
Passengers riding backwards, though, see things
Otherwise — and must feel guilty about it;
When I turn and catch them looking, their eyes

Drop, and they assume a preoccupied
Air meant to mime some private train of thought.
Impatience? Funk? A half-wish for derailment?
(They don't have *you* waiting for them, smiling. . . .)
Our steady, legato impetus is barred
At regular intervals by metal poles
That fly by in a soon predictable
Tempo, echoed also by the sag and soar
Of highstrung staff lines hanging down between.
I keep looking for groups of eighth-note starlings
To give the gallop a tune, but none are there,
Nor ever even a rest, just a continuing
Inaudible rush, variably elastic
According to our speed, which hums the landscape
Into a final tableau of motion itself —
A thing so strangely still at its utmost —
The factories, ashheaps, stations, transports caught
In a fastness that wants to hold my eyes
In thrall and lock me up in sleepless dreams.
(Your voice is putting accents in the transit,
Pulling me toward you on a silken line —
And dreams   that ran   on time   were Vehicles-
For-Something-Else. . . . ?)

    *

My mind winks on again — yes, there's that river
We cross here now, the same and always different.
A breeze intangible to me suddenly
Wakes the trees and blows on the gray water,
Shriveling the surface into a kind of
Elephant skin. A chevron of migrant geese
Flies into it — bull's eye straight to the heart
Of twenty concentric spreading circles. Water,

Birds, trees, swerve: how is it possible
To be moved in so many ways at once?

*

Our conductor shouts the listened-for station.
Though I've kept to one spot, the place has changed.
That, along with the name, which, red letter by
Reverse red letter, rolls toward me. Our shared
News — and the rest is neither here nor there,
Is anywhere we both shelter, still moving
Toward deeper welcomes, reunions. This racing
Panic will stop, once it's reminded we are
The only place I really want to go.

At the Grave Of Wallace Stevens

Cedar Hill Cemetery, 21 March, 1978

"We should die except for death." And even then
We do? The brightness of this early sun's
One light with that other day, five decades now,
When you cleared your throat and took to words again,
Tossing off your metaphysical hurts like
Speech impediments.

The back-and-forth of light and breath wants to,
By tmesis, free contracted hopes in all
Uninsurable things; and let them be
No cause for cause's sake or pieties,
The welling spring, dumb tears, far gone in earth's
Bright particulars.

This simple stone, its ashen pink incised
With simple lilies and your easy name —
And hers, the household tokens you exchanged —
Faces eastward, where Hartford's towers daydream.
A cedar and a budding willow cast
Shadows on the graves

And grass, the last patches of fluent snow
Withdrawing into mud and air; as if
To say, Poverty, be changed to Poetry:
Let the veil be torn away, the weather cleared
For a green metathesis where lucid leaves
Damask this new ground!

Philosopher of one or two ideas,
Touching no strings that hadn't been given —

And all the notions you had had had had
From the first the gaiety of stammered baubles,
As a way to say hiho to blank zero,
Shouting down the void.

These sturdy upright burgher bedsteads with light
And shadow sharply ruled in granite tell
Their legends to a sky *bleu ciel* — a thing
As it is in itself, but translated
Into distanced thought that comes nearer
Rhyming sound with mind;

And clouds freely associating one
Into another, still play to your own
High theater, tropical, boreal,
Informing and deforming what you saw
As final mercy, but, for other eyes,
Less than final loss.

To draw a golden bead on the marginal. . . .
Can you be felt as patient with a bitter
Restorative, a lighter régime building
Ruins to replace what was not at first
Meant for ruin? (Ask, as though you stood in this
Place of numbered stones —

Which might be graves of ancestors in that
Low country of the mind, at the middle height
Of dark, warring with nature's war, Antares
Pendant on the night, the noted vireo
And corydalis weeping over the cold
Spurls of passing time. . . .)

The bluster, the tawny lions of other

Marches take their place in gentle order.
To feel the flaw as a widening melt
And hear the wind speaking along bright strings —
The sun's a hat to be put on and then
Lightly doffed to you.

If it's still right to "like words that sound wrong,"
Take these to sleep on where you rest, under blue
Featherweight shadows, your tireless vigil now
The highway's self-renewing whisper, far
And near: endlessly it keeps revolving what
Time has written down.

Tanagra

In that day, even so moderate a ware
As you foreknew that laws like gravity's
Had rippled your stance in streamlike drapery
And fixed your earthen gaze on Theban stars.
Since you were cast to see as sculpture sees,
Change you cannot support, you will ignore,
Memento of future but still classic terrors,
The darkening pull down perpetuity.
That myth invoked, assume it as one more
Mantle. Too near to breath to choose the dead,
You help the traveler ford the dream he dreads,
Who stand in fluted robes on modern shores,
A single column, capital your head,
That bears the pondered weight of what we are.

Two Places in New England

I

Out on the speechless white plain
The snowshoes shush no sound unless their own.
Blue with no ice-clouds silent on high,
Aeronautic blue clear to the pole;
And a polar bloom infuses the fields.

Dry and watered grist, bear the weight.
Keep the record of each cross-hatched step.

A dozen half hoops,
The barbed raspberry canes
Anchored in snow, a wicker the dustiest
Brown rose.
No waxwing or winter wren nimbly stationed
On the stubble's threaded glaze; or on
The thick brakes of underbrush at field edge.
Strawy nearer weeds stand stoic
Over the snow, beside fallen bright berries,
Blooddrops in beaded spoor:
Some dainty velvet pelt, brown by black chevron,
Taken by a hawk, by an ermined owl,
Scripture on wing.

The bare beech, carven and muscular:
At each meeting of limbs a crater
Filled with snow, grails of light.
Will it always be damson bristle on the hills,
The trees and brush galena-bright in sun,
With jaggedly branched white birches singled out
Among them, frozen lightning-bolts

Shot from the ecliptic's great crossbow?

Winter, know, be, and say more than this
Intricate featureless plain of ice,
Shadowed by hemlock,
The needles' tight black plan,
Weeds their own monument,
Seeds their shorthand,
And, on snowslope façades up the rocks,
Scatterings of tiny scythes,
The split beech husks, twisted
Apart, opened, emptied, made past.
Winter, timeless machine, cold presence of the past —
A cold that is polar and blue, in the pastures and snowfields.

II

The fresh-rinsed rural chrysalis breaks open —
A wing, two wings, trying their fitness to the wind.
The air develops, but not stirs the gravestone,
A motto's Doric, sampler truth,
The marble vigil of a willow standing downcast,
Even in New England, above an antique urn.

Yet we only look and pass.
That a willow would be yellow
All in cascade over the brook
Where wobbling hoses and vocal jellies murmur,
Water; or bluegreen swords have risen,
Equinox germinator, from corms under mud;
And I take this sighting of you
In lost profile against the field —
It comes down to water, and things best made.

Water brought them, the builders and rebuilders —

Threshold to rooftree, shingle or clapboard.
"Trouble to build and rebuild the spring!"
Says the durable warbler coming back:
More subtle homespuns for a nobler nest,
Glovelike, to cradle the fragile prospects in.
Tireless burden of returning
Travelers, skill renewed on veteran wings:
Like a molding made of sound and motion,
Egg-and-dart, egg-and-dart, frames the air.

Naïve catkins, pollen-dusted;
Gold of an hour stayed in stacks of forsythia.
Light, be laid like malleable leaf
On polished branches, heraldic buds.

Side by side, across the springy compost,
We find the path again;
Past a broken toadstool circle,
Ghost meats and umber gills, a scattered henge.
Jack-in-the-pulpit back in the shadows
Of a cedar grove is holding forth to show the way —
And what crisper gesture now, spathe and spadix,
Than your green- and white-ribbed flourish?

Here: a rocky seat beside the flood.
At tips of leaves let beads of water-glass
Gather in the terrestrial sphere.
If rivers keep their history,
They keep it silent, all the liquid knowledge
Reworded in one kindly play —
Light on the water, on trees — a face —
To be so chancy, a burden so great —
Letting some things go — that others come —
Taking and giving speech away — the various light.

One to One

Unwrap the message hidden in a wound
Or a word: a branching spray of avowals, cut,
Massed, left to glide deathward in a vase. . . .
Face to face, a match, together until we choose;
And afterwards as well, isn't too much to hope for.
Still no sign of the chance to balance off
Independence and devotion — the armature jangled,
Door- and telephone-bell, errand, project,
A wave hello-goodby on the fraying wing.
Unmeasurable, the drag of countered origins,
The wind-chill factor, circumstantial walls.
There's always been a question, too,
Of satire mixed in with the mortar
Of our homemade, honeyed, subfusc nougat.
Faithful in your detachment, clear-eyed, marooned;
This you reserve to me — the person in the round,
A dark, and then the light side of the earth,
Warmth that spreads at a touch, as at dawn;
The play, the heft and pungency. Prized.
Best, I think, to leave chiaroscuro alone.
(And classify your cub or mooncalf name
Along with much else so sacredly banal
It has to take the reasonable vow of silence.)
A fresh effort sends me prospecting for clues,
Browsing in your empty study, paneled
With research and labor, leather, faded gold,
Patriarchal tobacco. Lamplight does and doesn't
Sum up a mind's household. Nor are you among those
Most at ease when being photographed or described.
In no uncertain terms, spleen, tinder,
Everready rejoinder when a mood strikes,

Head in flames, the shaft breaking smartly in two.
Your turn or mine to lay it out again,
How the all-intent have trouble conceding even
The clearest-cut foul, the pang's too sharp? Who,
When the smoke clears this time, will be missing
In action? One half, contracted to an unavoidable sky.
By magic you come back, gleam and scattered debris;
Pencil in hand, the cigarette sketching gestures
As gauze floats upward, unfurled, as the sun
Goes down. Free of one more day; and how much striving.
Remains the tireless need to be reimaged,
Where we were, where we are, the wide-ranging seesaw
Of the team, in full array, a full-blooded portrait.
(What questions don't dissolve in a green-brown gaze.)
Focus: the doorframe opposite, by three-quarter light,
Aplomb poised on the balls of your feet, the elbows
You nurse, and — just this once — the gravest of smiles.
The album fills, it grows substantial;
Superseded, replaced, updated, changed —
The candid, casual arrangements made.

Prime Minister in Retirement

Is, and has been raining several days.
Dull as rain, our plates of tarnished pewter
Line the walls. The tea — and fine Earl Grey's —
Has cooled inside her cup; it doesn't suit her.

Past, present, they boil down to much the same,
Don't they? Yesterday (and every) we read.
I'd say the future made less sound a claim:
Bonds are promised gold, not gold; and "lead"

In print's no more than scrip until a voice
Or context has determined whether it
Commands or means base metal. Speech is choice —
Home rule. I've made mine and weather it.

Cornwall

Sun rising at your back,
Cross the dry bed of the Tamar;
Wheels whisking the road behind
Unroll the land like carpet.

No poet, Cornwall?
None to praise the velvet pastures
With hand-hewn cows, couchant
Among purslane, granite and sorrel;

The faraway hillside meadow where
Sheep no bigger than rice grains graze,
Feeding, feeding like aphids
By the blasted pine and stunted oak?

St. Piran, patron of miners,
Come down in the shape of a sea-gull,
Crucified on your trim white wings,
Your halo bright as the top of a tin!

Bless the wolfram dug for treasure
At Castle-an-Dinas, heaped up there
Beside the brick stacks belching forth
Smoke-gouts, a wreath to heaven.

And do you take away the pagan stain
From the dolmens of Mufra and Chun,
The monoliths in the parish
Of charitable St. Buryans?

Best loved of his grandsire Alfred,
AEthelstan took this for England,
He tried to: lengthy Anglo-Saxon
Wrangles in the witenagemot.

"By Pol, Tre and Pen,
You may know the Cornish men."
But not one now will crawl nine times
Against the sun and through a stone

Ring, to be cured of rickets;
And today a boy was broken, died —
Stealing eggs from sea-gull nests,
He fell on the rocks at Falmouth.

And another struck by a black bolt
Flung down through high-tension lines —
Green glass fixtures afire with sun
Climbed recklessly among.

The spiked hawthorns all remember,
Some flushed pink as though with wine,
Blent with the high, savage hedgerows
That cicatrize the fields.

Remember, too, the sturdy inns,
Each with its peruke of thatch —
Trelawney, The Pillars, The Badger,
Smugglers, Three Pilchards, The Sloop —

And the sea-mists that lost to view
One lighthouse in St. Ives Bay.
The holiday-makers paced and paced,
And stared uncomprehendingly

At outdoor trays of turbot, cod,
Conger, dogfish, ray and skate.
(Cornish wrestlers at Agincourt:
And this is the English Riviera.)

Sun declining, but there's still time
To push down to the toe of the county,
Tipping into the Atlantic, O
The cliffs and sea-pinks at Land's End!

No magic if by a trick of light
And cross-hatched waves, the souls
Of the drowned move on the water,
Film-like now in purple shrouds.

They pace, call out, flail their arms
Backward into the deep; and they surely
Have telegrams for long-erased names
Who didn't drown, though will have died.

One changing-color silhouette
Has guessed the shores you left behind;
And knows the course, the sun-road down,
One last anchor in Dingle Bay;
Then out to the edge of the world:
Here There Be Monsters, and your home.

Maine Real Estate

Is hardship renewal? The cold waves
Keep coming in, little restrained
By islands offshore, where they ride
Ringed around by small, stripped-down craft.

Every lookout gazes seaward;
A whole township ignoring the signs
Nailed to walls and porches — a sale,
A July sale on houses. Mist

Rises from the lawns, stalling in the elms;
Shingle slumps, white paint scales, as though
Some genie steamed up from his oil-lamp
Had waved a fist and shouted, Collapse!

Dockside the Maritime Academy's
Grandest classroom sits at anchor,
Drawing a cadet up the gangplank,
His face deadpan, like the face

Of the infantryman a century
At ease on the green, forward inclined,
Granite rifle by his side.
No attention paid. Each citizen

Is visibly minding his business
Even when, reflexively, he
Barks out an "Afternoon"
To others on foot, who nod and pass.

What high, stinging whine gives it away —
That all, the most skeptical,
The most assured, are expecting news?
Word may come with the fog; cocooned

In a morning paper; or brought by the stranger:
Something else that must be borne. . . .
Briny droplets tingle in suspension;
The screen door of the general store

Reliably slams behind the postman,
Who stops, squints, tips back his cap
To catch, where it has broken through,
The pallor of the northern sun.

Audience

Electric arcs describe your mind,
Casual as it wants to be.
Your sweeping periods toll with light
And draw your subjects through a maze:
Their power flows from this small cell.

It's more a throne-room than a cell,
You say. The bars put you in mind
Of music's polyphonic maze —
Though time, the signature you'd be
Void without, is measured here by light.

Melody's insubstantial   light
As air   each note a honeyed cell
Golden wholes   O harmonic bee
In tune with that collective mind
Dance directing as through a maze

To fragrant rooms evolved to amaze
With walls finely built   for delight
Is intricate no less than mind
Like flowers construed cell by cell
Music plays us as we want to be

A program that's too rich, maybe,
For every day — but there was a maze
Once, in England. . . . Trapped in a cell
Of privet; and my head went light;
Knew it was sunstroke but didn't mind. . . .

Beamed through a maze of cells the mind
Weighs just more than light   let it be

The Outdoor Amphitheater

Those first scenes, lapidary, paintbox bright:
The climb down, half circle
By concentric half circle, opening
On to wherever the beginning is — .
The mists lift, run before the sun,
Retreat, and shrink into the trees.
Now, it's the public park;
And I am standing by myself, inside
The amphitheater.
Picture a grassy stage on a low rise, opposite some
Old wooden bleachers stained leaf-green —
But when I begin to see them
(Somewhere between ages six and fourteen),
Already weathered to a pale olive.
'52? '53? Memory's hide-and-seek.
Around then, the days you saw little girls
Dressed like dolls — hairribbons, pinafores trimmed
In rose-red rickrack — and boys wearing navy shorts
Held up by suspenders, in warm weather
(Which came early that far south), Easters or
Summer afternoons, when people, whole families,
Their friends and distant relatives,
Went to the outdoor amphitheater.

The idea hard to get in focus is not how things
Looked but how the look felt, then — and then, now.
That grassy cradle had the appeal, first,
Of its agreeable siting and landscaping:
A fresh green plot enclosed by ranks of trees;
Sometimes a few clouds floating overhead
(Compare with the vague "idea" mentioned above).

Oyster-gray clouds, April week-ends;
But then, almost always the ceiling broke
Up into sunlight later in the day —
A fine-screened, copper-gold afternoon sun,
Which stayed bright till nearly everybody
Had gone home, leaving the picnic debris,
All the plates and cups — paper but surprisingly
Functional — the ice-cream sticks and mimeo programs. This
Then had to be collected and carted away
By an old man who used a — did it have a name?
A sort of stabbing stick; a stabber. He never attacked
The litter with much enthusiasm
Or worked longer than, if that, half an hour.
So, there I am, sitting on the lowest,
Most splintered rung of the bleachers,
Talking to him the while.
I might be bubbling down (no straw needed) a 7-Up,
The process punctuated now and then
By a burp of sweet, eye-closing tear-gas.

Did he see the show, or hear the choir? No,
Never cared to. His job was just to tidy up.
Soon's that was done he could get home.
Which was where *I* ought to be. What was I doing
Hanging around here by myself anyway, say?
But I say nothing. A white wad
Goes to his brow, wrinkled and dark-shining. . . .
And then he fades away, gets dim and sepia
And lost. And the page turns to something else,
The dancing, music, speeches, and the plays.

The plays. What didn't we see — remember *Our Town?*
Yes, and *A Midsummer Night's Dream,*
Staged on Midsummer's Day. (And there

May have been — a little late for May Day — a May
Pole Dance, as a curtain-raiser.)
The Hermia, blonde, pretty, and
Lysander decided to pair off that summer;
Working together on the play had settled it.
He was the captain of the track team; she —
Nothing special, but interested in Dramatics.
As actors, no great shakes, but with
Nature backing up the magical lines,
They played at least the love scenes perfectly.
(Later they married and moved out of state.)
I wish there were some way to prove, now, that
They went back, the night of the performance,
To the amphitheater; kissed, stifled laughter,
Waiting darkly invisible till the moon rose. . . .
Does soft, silver light dissolve a danger,
And bring them safely through this? Suppose someone out
Of work, and looking for trouble, some thug, came up —
What then? But in the early '50s that
Was unheard of, unthinkable.
Which they knew or rather just assumed. (Half the fun
Was a fine carelessness — wouldn't the play always
End with Titania firmly enthroned again?)

"Small" and "painful": how the two can be felt as one
Thing welded together. He grows taller
And stronger, trying to force apart the tandem;
And one bright morning is graduated.
Every June, Commencement Exercises
For the high-school, weather permitting, were
Held outdoors in the amphitheater.
Ours finally, my class's turn!
We sat there hot and damp in the heavy
Black humanist garb, with those absurd mortarboards
And trembling tassels. Ludicrous; and all the more

If you happened to sport grim, black-rimmed specs
Like those that had devolved on me
During the long assault on Knowledge. And my spoils?
The Valedictory, an address spoken at the end
Of our ceremony. A one-off and no doubt pointless
Performance, which I sweated over weeks
Beforehand, writing, crumpling up, writing. . . .
I must find something that would harmonize
A sense of farewell with aspirations toward the future.
No undertaking for the fainthearted;
But then, the members of my family
Had never appreciably lacked conviction;
Nor was this the first time I had been magnified
Within the hot focal point of audience attention.

No, my first stage appearance came much earlier —
Brief and, to judge by the response,
A flop. Where my teacher got the notion
That an eight-year-old, even with a clear,
True alto, accurate and on pitch, could
Put over two high-toned songs, one religious, one
Patriotic, please tell me. Earnestly performed;
Politely received. That was the interpreter's
Vocation, then, its own reward?
I did think I'd given a good account
Of my songs, myself: let that be *enough.* And yet,
I wouldn't, plausibly, have scorned
Instant acclaim had it been forthcoming.
I took my seat while the applause thinned out
And the next performer sallied up to the mike.
Through puzzlement and flooding eyes
I could see only — green. Leaves and branches
Like flotsam downstream the rushing immense
River of sky. And then, nothing.

Those days, mostly I was the spectator,
Taking it all in. Taking, but also giving:
For the true audiences would work hand in hand
With the performer, their puppet, "pulling for him";
Who must in turn put half, the more vigilant half
Of his mind second-row center —
A benign, inventive form of self-appraisal.
(And a strenuous task. Can there be some
Who *only* want to perform, and never to watch?)
Not that such issues preoccupied me back then;
I simply lived their force, avid to share
In the alchemy, the uncanny teamwork of stagecraft.
Example: that student circus
From a small university in Florida —
That stands out. Those demented and inspiring acts!

Jugglers, tumblers, clowns, daredevil tightrope artists
Who danced on high, to appearances unaware that one
False move meant curtains for the pitiful, broken
Star, flattened and paralyzed on the grass.
No, it was only the fun they felt, or seemed to.
As for the garish costumes, the tinsel, plumage,
And rhinestones — not to let them be transformed
By mental footlights into an orient richness:
It would have been cloddish, a betrayal
Of the all-expansive theatrical spirit.
Go along or not with the enchantment? Ours to choose.
Nearly everybody preferred, as I remember,
To be pleased; banged their palms together and went home
With aerial feats spinning in the brain, magic
Tableaux, and how many zany escapades to dream on —
The lesson borne in indelibly that,
Should a number come a cropper, complete fiasco
Can often be subverted by a skillful clown.

Other thrills: there was that chorus, visiting from —
Outer space, it's tempting to think.
The Wagner Chorale, was it? Anyway,
Two hundred voices' unearthly precision in
Modernized but ravishing renditions
Of Orlando di Lasso, Handel, Bach;
Bliss. And then, art versions of folk tunes, black
And white, both belted out with crack syncopation
And pressurized swells, some dynamite sforzandi
That might have brought the rafters down,
But as it was, settled for five-part lightning bolts
("What You Going To Do When The World's On Fire?")
Flung upward to the firmament among lofty
Cumulus clouds and ramps of golden sun.
For the young, latest convert to harmony, it
Was much as if a wingèd envoy with beetled brows stared
From the recruiting poster, index aimed straight on,
Above the caption: "The Angelic Host Needs You!"
Well, volunteers beat the draft — in block print, I signed.

What else? Oh yes, some traveling entertainers,
A vaudeville, with hoofers and comedians, called
THE FAMOUS . . . somebodies.
I do remember they arranged to have the name
Of the revue, in big, separate, bright
Red letters, put out in front of the stage.
I had come early, to watch them, racing
Around in frantic sweat, set up.
Say there, would I give them a hand?
THE FAMOUS letters — if I would just move
Them, in order, out front. You bet!
But, in the thick of the task, an idea,
A silly one, took possession of me:
To think of myself as the letter "I," and then

Link up with some of the consonants (just
About my height), to see what I could spell.
The result? Telegraphic chips,
Necessarily; but here's a sentence
I remember liking and repeating aloud:
IF   IM   IT   IT   IS   I.
(Ending up a unit again, as it
Had to have been.) "Places," they called,
Waving me to my seat, all further assistance
Snared on the jazzy opening line of the saxophone.

The show itself was "certifiably" funny,
Even though the big-city, for-the-birds
Wisecracks went winging well over my head.
This much was plain: some day I must
Get to the bottom of them. On the spot —
Well lighted within it — plans began to be laid.

Just because it's at the other end of the scale,
I'll bring up here another gathering —
The revival meeting, a regular feature
Of our summers. The one I single out,
Not unusual for the fervor it bred in us
(This was John Wesley country, after all),
Sticks in my mind because of the sincerity,
Youth, and out-of-the-ordinary handsomeness
Of the preacher. "Almost Persuaded," ran the hymn,
But, in truth, we were altogether persuaded, won
Over to guilt and salvation, washed clean
By the blood and weeping our own real tears.
Time has dried them. But not the memory
Of his fiery sermon on the coming apocalypse.
Who didn't recognize the crushing likelihood
Of what he proclaimed? The Time Was At Hand.

Not one of us but had heard Gabriel
Heatter on the radio warm to the subject
Of Korea, the Red Menace, the Domino
Theory. . . . Those veterans listening
Who'd had their combat baptism in the Pacific
Theater paused to reflect on total war, the Atom
Bomb, Asian Fanaticism, Kamikazes,
And Communism. We'd do well to look ahead.
First, lay down stores in the basement — canned goods,
Water, ammunition; but more important still,
Get ready to meet our Maker.
The worry hovering over me always was
My reluctance to greet Millennium.
Must the world *burn* to bring the Kingdom in?
An event all too easy to picture,
Blending, indeed, bleeding into what I
Had already gleaned here and there about the eternal
Brimstone climate of Hell, where the world kept
On horribly ending in never-ending flame.
Sitting there on the grained wood bleachers, hot,
Mosquito-tormented, my eyes transfixed by his
Ardent, sweating face, suddenly I knew
How it would come to pass: His hand would strike,
The night sky turn supernova, sun-white
Beams transfigure all below, as atom after atom
Gave up the fiction of matter, form, the fallen
Rain of vindictive fire tipping earth, houses, trees,
Dominos over into the flowing unspeakable
Flamebows of fission tided to whatever stars
Had escaped the earthly and solar catastrophe: this
Would be the millennium, when the Kingdom came.

So, when the preacher made his pitch, when he
Numbered our errors and omissions, we listened;

Choked back emotion, repented; believed.
That the knowledge could be sustained, renewed,
Become the seed of marked and saving change
Was the illusion. That, for one, the wife — in pain,
Outdone — might at some point lean up on an elbow
To say it wasn't working out, and could they talk?
That the husband who felt trapped in his job, his house,
Might at last try to come to terms, withdraw,
And make a new beginning. That
The child who couldn't get himself across
To those arbitrary figureheads fearfully in charge
Might find a way this time.
No, it never quite sticks. The feeling holds a day,
A week, then becomes a memory, and then — .
By the time the schoolhouse doors swing
Open in the fall, everything's back to normal.

Migrating bird summerbound for the Gulf
And South America, a late autumn passage
Low over the park in midafternoon
Spreads wide the mapped, down-on view of open
Space, brown grass across whose expanse
The tiny figure walks his diagonal,
An everlasting newcomer's minute progress
No moment in your fleet, watch-jewel eye. . . .
Not this, but some unwritten score
Of high and low in the green cabinet
A child takes for his serious playhouse,
Ground bass of pain whelmed over in a free-for-all
Of whisper, hue, scent, savor, grain,
Composed, the slow length of a homeward mile,
My study. November: never a hint of snow,
But downcast leaves, temperatures, cold trek
Through the dark house, bare ruin of a theater

On my way — those signs told that the solstice
Previews, under whose direction, would now begin.
Was winter's gift to simplify, cut back, unravel thread
By thread the tissue of what summer knew?
Openings and closings and openings. . . .
Now perhaps, but could I then condemn the wish to mount up,
Up past the holding patterns and wingborne flight to a stage,
A new year, fruit and flower dancing together
In breezes outside any fixed global compass?
If the boy could stay, and stay dissatisfaction,
Each step not draw him farther on,
Always back to his own small room,
The creaking furniture, lessons,
Chores, his present, and his distant future;
If the cloud ceiling could break, and he be
Gathered in — . But the time isn't at hand.
Stock still, he waves upward, goodby, goodby;
Lets the hand drop; looks around him. And what
Does the player do in an empty theater?
Almost empty. But see, the neighbor dog
Comes sidling up with barks and wags; then stops,
Takes a position; and
Leaves behind a reminder that we are
Earthly clay. On which, to heart's content, dwell
Those who will, those who can.

One blue-and-gold April my older sister was
Crowned Queen of the Beauty Pageant.
All over the park early-flowering
Dogwoods hovered against the shaded green background
Like new galaxies in hushed explosion.
My sister wore a ball-gown, the pastel satin
Odd but touching, there, out of doors. She laughed
And sobbed energetically while, with equal energy,

The MC squared his shoulders under a rented
White jacket, coughed into his fist, and thrust
A sheaf of red roses and carnations
Into her arms. Sweet, familial pride
Flooded through me; and, besides, people said
We looked so much alike. . . . So, the Pageant
Concluded, last applause subsiding, all
The friends and relations rose, nodded and greeted
Each other, handshakes and kisses bestowed crisscross
Around, signs of a shared contentment that
One of the community had been recognized
As beautiful, the youthful sovereign of Spring. . . .
These were habits, too, of seasoned husbandry; for,
Since that good held in common never flourishes
Without the single, uncommon effort —
However dreamborne and momentary seeming —
Palms and applause must come down handsomely;
Gifts and promise of every kind be acknowledged,
Take the platform and stand firm under the weighty
Crown, knowing its meaning: that the assembled will
A continuance; that this stage not be the last;
And that the performance move on from strength to strength.

FROM

Notes from a Child of Paradise

1984

I.

One

In the middle of everything a voice
From the depths of the house sings out for me
To pick up the phone. Good news? New work-sheets
Watch the interrupted reader raptly
Dreaming on them start wide awake and leave
The bedroom-study (inset here one bright
Window on April 15, deep blue skies,
Branches, flowers of the cornelian
Cherry, a yard glazed with mud; and any
Number of thoughtlike, all-changeable clouds).

At the desk again, a curling snapshot
Of you, leaning against the spine of my
Old Grandgent *Commedia* makes me want
To dub under it the laughter-silvered
Tones that just now firmed up plans to visit. . . .
Ash and pearl, a seabeach in the Northwest;
Your trim sylphide body five years younger,
And calm dry gaze at least five older than
The 24 of then. . . . Heartbeat, answer:
Must part of us always remain intact?

Wind-tossed clouds, shaking branches, black spring mud,
Take up the note, new anachronisms
For the lighthearted pair, courtly beneath
Technologies, garlands of ice and fire,
Their stories indisseverably wound
Around transport in an age of airships —
So that the first vehicles gliding down
From heaven to this field where I coax home
Figures for love's arriving stars and tears,
Its scalds and wordlessnesses, are airborne.

II.

The balancing wings of hendiadys
Shuttle me back to 1964,
When, anticipating Dante's, that's right,
*Hepta*centennial, a special course,
Dark Wood to Rose of Fire in one quick spring,
Enthralled this receptive language major;
Who, having Time-spanned earlyward a week
Of centuries, vacation come, would next
Branch out in Space — a first, short trip abroad.
So: Kennedy Air France flight lounge. *And there*

You were. . . . What must a young woman — tawny,
Silk-straight, Beatnik-style hair free-flowing far
Down the back; wrapped in a Bogart trenchcoat;
A Camel in the left hand, Gore Vidal's
Julian in the fine right; brown eyes well up
To Provençal standard (say, Peire Vidal's) —
Have thought of our weedy assembly, some
Fifty loafer types, all in a summer
Program of French studies (language practice
Among the papal stones of Avignon)?

No need to guess. This much I know: right then,
Even before takeoff, the foreshortened
Transatlantic arc toward dawn, and that long
Paris-to-Midi-*Mistral* trainride, when
Our startled eyes met and glanced off, glanced, met
Through jokes traded at all the world's expense
(Excepting the suave, francophone elect),
Before our timed-to-the-second *descente*
To find our summer hosts (the French rail lines
Are notably not late) — I'd fallen hard.

III.

That secret, though, played Papageno-With-
Buttoned-Lip. There was, I gathered, someone
Else, a fact to surprise no escort who
Had dwelt the length of a held breath on those
Features, or that voice between grave and gay. . . .
And if I, for my part, had just come out
From under six months of scarifying
Lovesickness (smiles, hugs, promises — he was
What I didn't then want to call a tease),
The case seemed to have escaped your notice.

Among your friends were men with men friends, but —
Somehow you didn't see *me* in that light.
Too mooncalfish, was I, hanging on your
Least word and gesture; too understanding
When dissatisfaction with his letters
Showed through? Could be. I never presumed, just
Studied to please, played whatever cards of
Comedy and book lore I could muster.
Lessons in love are poetry, who doubts?
The Muse turns down uneducated louts.

Nightly the autodidact crammed till three.
Some more Italian (which you crisply spoke);
The sinuous *dizains* of Scève's *Délie;*
Arcadia (for the Countess of Pembroke) —
Now which of us fell for the pains I took?
Pure bliss beside the Fountain of Vaucluse,
Recycling figures Petrarch used to use:
Her golden-arrowed eyes, O frost that burns. . . .
Great Freud! Since you teach men self-disabuse:
Who makes us house our loves in Grecian urns?

XIV.

No letters? The clerk gave a pitying
Italianate shake of the head as I
Turned, slunk back, pushed open wheeling glass doors
That broke in pieces gold bars of morning
Light, refracted javelins hurled through crowds
Thronging the dim arcades. *Stop choking. Time*
To wake up, forget her. A third person
Had thrust into the deepest of my dream —
Damn, even fools tire of playing the fool.
This one had red blood, was twenty, hungry.

A long hour in the subaqueous glow
Of the throne room or swim tank that housed
Young *David*, celestially gymnastic —
Copies in plaster of whom still preside
Over a million knickknack collections
In the free world, our first teenage idol.
His outsize hand lolled in all innocence
Against the lean flank, like a slingshot just
Having let fly its missile to the brow.
Lodged there, this opened a piercing third eye.

Which now would help one see the city plain?
Humanist Contra Naturam, a speech
Cognate with city life, must sometimes reach
New heights where sacred aims appear profane.
The probing mind fixed on the patterned stones
Of a square crossed, or breaking free to stare
At Babel building far, or nightspot near —
The clientèle lilting in foreign tones
And offering friendly help for what disturbs —
Began to practice Second Nature's verbs.

XIX.

"Now I am one-and-twenty," so I heard
Myself think. Too hectic to take a bow
When in Rome the day had come to confer
Its ghostly toga on me, here was time
To ponder a civic status needing
Two Augusts more to seem at all confirmed.
Back to home and country. And to a last
Year of school, which, though senior-level, felt
Retarded, the mid-Atlantic limbo
Rushed to agree with him who rode it out.

Now, with just twice his span of consciousness
Under my hat, should I envy, pity,
Mock that fledgling life? No more, I guess, than
Any other other person's. The bulk
Of his archive has been settled on me;
And sift as I will its strange content keeps
A far-gone quality I recognize
Yet would no sooner try to reassume
Than squeeze into the vintage jeans he wore,
Or reread his latest favorite book.

Now, I know, will have been that misnomer
That rarely holds the fort for long — so brief
A stay it couldn't always accustom
Its golden hoard of clairvoyance to all
We might have meant to one another. See
How slowly we move to be reconciled;
How stoutly jetstream contention baffles;
How reluctantly we touch ground, even
In the tall city where, back then, I could
Visit — believing or not — *The World's Fair.*

XXI.

Just under halfway on, a decade stands
Out as itself; gets hawked from the newsstands;
Then scores in deeper; and pockets the dice.
(Already we'd seen a president fall,
Killed by random madness.) Then, late that fall,
Rumblings from California; for you
Had gone back West, "the Berkeley transfer." Like
Our generation's Best Minds used to like
To say, the San Francisco scene was what
Was happening, for life and style alike.

I still don't quite imagine you out there.
The Terrace. Marx-tinted glasses. And there
Was, you wrote, a paved walk jammed with tables —
Leaflets, manifestoes, world-seen-red. Plus
An antic Harpo-Groucho fringe A-plus
Students like you smiled at as you passed.
Politics mattered. Sex and pop-songs too:
"We are the LPs that we listen to."
In residence were Ginsberg and Baez,
Setting things up — to mention only two.

Yes, but Leary'd dropped in (or out) and joined
Forces with heads for whom a decent joint,
Once, had been enough. (Capsule sacrament,
A.k.a. LSD, I'm afraid
We mostly bought your propaganda: "Frayed
Electric Chord, Illumination, turn
Us on!" Legally, by U.S. Mail, came
A trip from you. Taken. . . . *Then time oncame*
A skewed movie   hot crestrisen rainbow
Sirenbeam   Homing in the dreamers came)

I.

Two To run their small boat faster, these two
Sails, tension and release in balance,
From pole to pole alive, send it scudding
Across the sea under a genial gust
Of animal spirits. . . . Silver light. Now
He wakes to ask what embodiment she
Is beside him here, smooth-shouldered, lapped
In sleep, a nimble, complementary warmth.
This time is not the same as yesterday's.
He swallows, fights the tug toward tenderness
As her eyes falter open, comprehension
Welling up, to rest on him. Lips part
In smiles, the first of many similar.
A stretch underlines them both; rustle
Of bedclothes, limbs, murmured tones, whispers. . . .

For her, expanses of feeling: contentment, salt
Certainty of having become overnight
A pair, twin names caught up in one blaze.
He's the awkwardly gentlest so far, gazing
Down in sturdy calm from a propped elbow,
Hair ruffled in contrary directions,
The coals of ardor breathed on, glowing.
Added, a bluish shading when she counts
The handful of conversations left them, a short
Week to unfurl the new dispensation. . . .
She hears silent urgings, maternal accents,
The same that last night saw to getting in
Something for breakfast; the wish to give pleasure.
Muffins, café au lait poured like tribute.
Love flares across a bowl of oranges.

IV.

Graceless to mingle honeymoon with class,
Apartment-hunting, all that our move entailed;
But soon enough we'd settled into place,
(Whitman, *Song of the Exposition*) "install'd
Amid the kitchen ware" — a furnished flat
Off Riverside Drive. No, *fur*bished: grandiose
And fraying, formerly salon of, what,
An 1880s Romanesque château
Hacked into single and double pieds-à-terre.
You entered through the bedroom, paused, then stepped
On grassgreen carpet into a high chamber
With a big marble fireplace carved in rapt
Mêlée: coquilles, acanthus, spiral pillars,
And central triton puck whose branching thighs
Unscrolled in supple coils to either side.

Here we unpacked. And made up a true-romance
Story about our Gotham-Gothic home.
Yet with your sister Liza's color prints
Hung on the walls, genteel bordello gloom
Began to lift. . . . Remember when we sat
Down to our first real dinner, tall windows
With leaded lozenge mullions letting late
September dusk and, sure, some long-stemmed candles
Play two tones on our table, flickering
In time with Mozart (K. 622 —
His warmest work, did I agree? Your "theme song.")?
I do. . . . So topics would arise: Watteau,
Bergman, the *Sonnets,* a speech of Reverend King.
And always we knew (knew almost audibly)
That U.S. fire was tearing through Hanoi.

VII.

Changes: they argued of and for themselves, as
Hemlines soared to write another chapter
In the red book of hotline revelations,
Airwaves spinning with the London latest
That fans in pea-jackets shook their mare's-nest
Curls to, then dropped, to play a California
Riff on new guitars from some oldtime
Blues or country tune. Ten thousand changes
Past, it's an irretrievable sensation,
The glee that dawned when every day spit out a
New kink, new look, or epoch-making album.
For once behind the times, New York mostly
Served as a clearing-house, eager to welcome
Back what pioneers had left the Village
For good times on Telegraph Avenue.

In fact, Berkeley had folded, so your friends
Announced, who dropped in for an hour that late
November. The truly revolutionary
Core of the Movement had gone to Haight-Ashbury.
A winning spirit of Love and Inner Light
Ignited in San Francisco should spread from there
To the whole world; and stop all wars. We listened,
The mendicant brothers' voices earnest with change
Of heart; and let thoughts play out a tendril
Revery, goldfish swarming into paisleys,
Meshwork mosaic laved downstream the music
Of change. . . . Outside, skies showed silver-gray
Above the sootstained buildings of the city.
And, through small rifts and tears in the cloud ceiling,
Scattered portholes of late, redeeming blue.

XII.

All right. If freedom wants to be fulfilled,
No doubt it needs a household to itself:
Ann finds a studio closer to school;
Al, a downtown crashpad in what's being called
The East Village, matrix of the new
Mystic-drug-and-social revolution
(Which can't be launched at uptown rental rates).
They promise they'll commute to see each other;
But as for classes, he simply doesn't go.
No problem. While his right hand dashes off
A few last papers ("Gautier and Baudelaire")
The practiced left twirls tight a cigarette
For impromptu meetings of the *Club
Des Haschischins*. What the A's received might owe
To special illumination, does he care?

He cares about the journey with closed eyes;
About varieties of mystic thought;
About perception, its portals flung wide
To rainwashed color, texture felt in the gut,
Proliferating symmetries, light figures
In the optic carpet, magic, music,
Philosophy at one with the heartbeat,
With the wild torque of the galaxy, dilate
Pupil, wheel within wheel. . . . Even the flower
Tendered by the smiling jeweled devi
Whose precinct's Tompkins Park encapsulates
(Its sunbright disc, its radiating petals)
That first love, the innovating starburst
Of creation, down to the tiny solar flock;
To earth; to flesh; and the mind perceiving all.

XIV.

In due course, I train uptown to check
On how you're coping. What's your news? Oh, nothing.
Well, your colleague's begun to show
His true colors. A bully like them all.
Fresh out, *Sergeant Pepper's Lonely Hearts*
Club Band drops to the turntable, spinning
Rueful fables of constraint and freedom.
And gives a hint of having anticipated
(After earlier successes) the slight
Disappointment we feel. Its jacket features
The stars, in psychedelic Salvation Army
Uniform, gazing down at what might
Be their own grave, bloodred hyacinths
Spelling out the name that launched ten million
Discs, and a raft of famous dead behind.

"The love that's gone so cold and the people . . .
And life flows on within you and without you."
You stretch, begin to do a little housework.
Is this the moment to note again how feeling
Tends to override its simplest settings?
The props, and maybe the actors, too, will seem
To matter less than the high voltage channeled
Through them; so that even here, as you stack
Records and papers, in faded shirt and jeans,
You are all you ever have been, ever.
A votary will need no gilded stage,
No ambrosial music, no holy terrors
To be caught up in a silken spin that makes
The conscript dancer sense his happiest role is
To foot a rough equivalent of The Dance.

XVI.

By Dante's subtle twinnings Purgatory
(That late-patristic timeclock metaphor he
Took as the gospel) finds its counterpart
In Mount Parnassus; and the labor art
Exacts from journeymen is figured in
His staggering climb from haplessness and sin
Up to celestial heights of expertise
And grace — which leaves him more than skilled to please
Angel and mortal alike in sacred meter.
Since Beatrice (though he doesn't meet her
Till Canto XXX) is saint as much as muse,
The pilgrim's and the poet's love must fuse.
If quests lead *to* the father from the son,
The second of these trinitarian
Canticles would form the Holy Spirit's bridge

Between those persons, through the . . . matronage
Of a stern, loving lady who has discarded
Flesh for spirit. In the lessons larded
Throughout the narrative, the pilgrim's taught
That bondage to base instinct must be fought;
What his heavenly mistress seems to ask is
*Dis*incarnation. When she takes to task his
Earthly amours, it's not mere jealousy,
No, but prophetic zeal to set him free
From all the downturned heaviness of nature. . . .
A lesson for the artist, too? The fate you're
Born to is only an early rung of that
Ladder of Vision or pealing Magnificat
Beyond the Spheres? No doubt. But look, here's sight:
Which sees the pilgrim still at middle height.

XXV.

Its spokes converging on the stapled hub
Of the Etoile, Paris wheeled into place
Below. Another turn, and then Orly.
(How many revolutions since, the one
Step by step preparing then has come
To seem respectable almost, a bookend;
But who in 1968 foresaw it?)
Step one: *l'affaire Langlois*. The founder of
The Cinémathèque was suddenly dismissed.
Sartre, the universitarians,
P.C. intellectuals and all
The filmic world joined forces to protest.
J'accuse's, posters, letters. Finally
Malraux, as Minister of Culture, acted
To reinstate the ineluctable.

Reason the Goddess smiled as left-wing praxis
Took careful note, and all of us bought tickets
For *Potemkin* and *October.* But now
Students here too began to feel they
Possessed a special gift of divination,
Restiveness, challenge, rage, their common fuel.
Targets: Vietnam partitioned by foreign
Fiat. Consumerism's python grip.
The "hospital society," which counted
Almost everyone by now, the poor,
The ghettoized, the sad, the numb, the mad.
Keep Southeast Asia safe at any cost
For Western anomie? The blinded leaders
Knew not what they did and must be helped
Or pushed to see the right; but soon, before

XXVI.

The plague had spread past hope of remedy.
Discourse volleyed back and forth between
Nanterre and Place Maubert, *Défense d'afficher*
The first restraint to crumble as the walls
Papered over with grievances and slogans,
The wise and ardent icons, Chairman Mao
And Che Guevara. For the first time in decades
The International assumption rang
True. And here was electric news from home:
Columbia had been taken over, shut
Down by the S.D.S. till further notice.
The gray sandstorm of a wire photo
Coalesced around a teenaged striker,
Feet propped on President Kirk's desk,
Puffing a cigar beneath a Rembrandt portrait.

Not since Berkeley, we thought. . . . But what about
Our friends — teachers, students, who might be caught
Up in the drama? Telephone parleys,
Expensive, curtailed, picked their way over
A minefield of conflicting sympathies.
Which tipped in favor of the protest once
Guards swept down and cleared the buildings, clubbing
Anyone too slow to dodge. For blood
Is still blood, however urgent the theory
That sheds it: I'd read my Camus and Rosa
Luxembourg. But didn't bother citing
Them to the *Comité de base*, whose next
Meeting announced plans for a clash of arms
With *Occident*, an ultra-rightist group.
Our chairman's eye locked with mine, amethyst

XXVII.

Glint from his spectacles anticipating
The chill contempt he'd feel for me when I
Voiced some objections fostered by "Bourgeois-
Humanist Conditioning." *Whereas*
A scientific grasp of social process
Should obviate the sentimentalism
Of weeping overmuch for those oppressed
Or killed while history accomplished what
Inexorable purposes it held
In store for the People. Merely incidental
People, I wondered? And whether these committees
Really much cared about the Vietnamese.
Wasn't, instead, the point here to recruit,
Indoctrinate, and train new Party members?
Disguise, deception, doctrinal dressing-down —

As techniques banal compared to what torture
And murder I knew had been performed before.
"No, I'm not in favor. I resign."
I walked out, bathed in cold sweat,
On my mettle, furious, my back tingling
Where eyes had drilled in before I closed
The door. . . . How easily this all told itself
To you when I collapsed on our sofa-bed.
The city lights began to pinprick on
Some twenty stories beneath our window. We
Curled up together, exchanging murmurs with no
Ballast of ideology or spleen.
A thick bat of bread on the sideboard.
Three francs' worth of anemones. A litre
Of *ordinaire* — which it was time to decant.

XXVIII.

News from Nanterre: a crackdown no less brutal
Than Columbia's. And then an echoic
Roar of support from the Quartier Latin.
Students ten thousand vocal marched against
The incarceration of their leaders, state
Repression. The Sorbonne closed its doors.
Shouting matches, harassment, and at last
A pitched battle, which deployed in slow
Motion, a liquid nightmare staged around
Collagist barricades thrown together
From lumber, capsized cars and paving stones.
The C.R.S., black-helmeted, with shields,
Goggles and nightsticks, swarmed from armored trucks,
Advancing through a fusillade of stones.
Protesters, in street clothes, fell down and bled.

Cries. Distant sirens. The faint burn
Of teargas drifted down to the 13e.
When quiet returned, I stealthily threaded
My way up toward the brooding Panthéon
And rue St. Jacques, wondering whether some new
Education sentimentale would be hatched
From this unrest. The tower of Ste. Étienne
Said, "Paris repeats herself, true, but the terms
Differ. . . ." A liberated Odéon
Now featured a round-the-clock debate
Open to whoever could make himself heard.
Groups or solos seized the platform, held it
Till hounded down by boos or *Merde!*'s: total
Dissent voiced in a total democracy.
(I still can't get that noise out of my ears.)

XXXIII.

It would be hardly truthful if I said
We boarded the ship without a qualm. The crest
Of each westward-breaking wave recapped
Many an intuition one was half
Willing to let roll back into the deep.
Distractions, though, were near, in case of need:
New *Pléiade* Prousts, our bodies, nightly toasts
To the shade of Bessie Smith, to Chairman Ho.
And still, I'd gaze for hours at the blue
Expanse, its shimmer-silver foils, to brood
Over Columbus and his voyage — not
How he managed it but *why* he felt the call.
Riches? Glory? Soon as pronounced, the words
Are snatched away in the wind. . . . Day four: I turn
To you, accomplice, *chère âme.* No joking dismissals?

(Tomorrow, ushered in by tugs and whistles,
Our right-on-time *United States* will find
The harbor's open door with, on one hand
 — Gothic and Machine Age linked together —
The triune Brooklyn Bridge, and on the other,
Lifting her verdigris torch straight up into
The arc of molten noon, Miss Liberté.
To them shall go salutes, loud homage from
The milling travelers, half-drunk with home
And looking for convenient icons to thank.)
For now, let sun, all fire and steamclouds, sink
Into its golden track; and evening call
The seaworn pair, who, up for a last stroll
On deck — he inwardly framing his, she hers —
Wish on two of the first and brightest stars.

IV.

Three Sunday mornings, stretching into the afternoon,
We would negotiate the day in bed.
Grapefruit, book review, coffee, telephone.

Snowcooled light through open shutters;
Copland from the speakers; always the ground-bass
Knowledge that tomorrow you'd trudge off

To that humdrum office job that meant nothing
At all to you; and I, in turn, to my classes.
Tonight? "Oh, Ed's coming over to read

The draft of a chapter from his novel." (Which,
Urged on by us, he will complete, dedicate
To us, and publish — but that came later.)

Meanwhile, my Paris pages have had the savoir
To find a nesting place in a bottom drawer;
And I've been kicked upstairs, yes, back to poems.

How to begin? Prowling the bookstores
And finding no epigones of Baudelaire,
I wondered whether someone might not still — .

Long since destroyed, a few early trials
Float back now in outline — with their subjects
When so equipped. Wasn't there one about you?

Or about a silence, a distance I felt sometimes
Between us. You were ensconced halfway across
The room, absorbed in reading *The Second Sex*.

The Siamese lately acquired crouched
Next to you, tail flicking. . . . And so on.
Nothing "mystique" in the cat, or of Jeanne Duval

In you. A mentor chosen consciously
Often dries up on the vine. Something else
Has presided — homegrown; looser; stranger.

VI.

Midwinter thaw. Abruptly it replays
Our meeting here three Februaries since.
Fire and ice, sleepless nights, short days

Restored, without notice shunted back
By sunfilled waterdrops spilling from
Rooftops, clearing streets and gutters. Black

Branches snowmelt bright in the park stir
And gauge the air. . . . Indoors again, we'll tug off
Galoshes, let them drain on newspaper,

The muddy dregs smear over stricken
War news headlines. So far, nothing avails,
Calls to Congressmen, marches. The sickening

Deployment of violence both here and over there
Gouges deeper into consciousness,
Unyielding as a game of solitaire.

— The backdrop for our youth. Would it leave
Us unscarred? (Reply withheld until old
Age comes bearing it, with a wrinkled reprieve. . . .)

Nearer horizons then: this summer we
Think of traveling West to visit your mother out
In Oregon; a longtime wish to see

Your childhood haunts and friends. Besides, we wanted
To drive overland, a motive in itself —
Iowa, Nebraska, Wyoming, the vaunted

Big Sky, exotic names that preserved some
Of the Pioneers' sunset splendor. Also,
Reading and liking *On the Road,* I'd come

To see its narrator Sal Paradise
(The Kerouac stand-in) as a late avatar
Of Whitman. Perpetual journeys: why not splice

VII.

Them onto our free-flowing Interstates?
Another neat idea already scooped:
For (this is next June) my scanner focusing

On the van passing by, the name of its make
Snapped into the foreground, brash as AM radio:
Open Road, trim designation of the myth

That fueled a seemingly inexhaustible
Stream of internal-combustion self-movers
Cruising behind, around and ahead of us — a myth

Well inside our awareness and inwardly
Rehearsed as rolling Ohioan fields
Slid along the greased, flexible ribbon

Of I-80. The last handful of images
From Philadelphia (our first landfall)
Thin out like a scrim over the present scene,

The spire of Independence Hall coinciding
With the steeple of a Lutheran church,
Urban brick with the squarecut barns

Painted brick-red and crisscrossed with chalk-
White trim. Watertower to silo, antenna
To windmill, the farms approach, swell,

And subside as we make steadily westward,
Just skirting Cleveland and Toledo, herds
Of us on our ten thousand errands,

The social contract here a matter of lanes,
Of life and death (since a heedless or hasty
Runover from slow to passing could kill how many

Independently cooperating citizens,
All mindful that the rule "Drive and let drive"
Arises from each one's having his fair destination).

XIII.

In Santa Fe the constellated night
Whose Dipper swings low as if to douse the desert.
For every star, three cicada voices, a sense

Of the world's orb turning through a mesh
Of sound and starlight. As many low roofs
And white houses as can be made out in darkness

From our hotel balcony represent the town,
Its trustworthy human scale. Close of day,
A day on foot through ochre dust, the bending

Streets of the Barrio de Analco. Timeworn
San Miguel. Arcades of the Governors' Palace.
On brown arms, silver and lumps of turquoise, smoothed

Pace of conduct, deliberate, fated, at one
With the cloudless sky transfixed by a single
Crossbeamed silver sun. Completeness, like the rounded

Snow of adobe. Reticence, like the shadows
In half-seen courtyards. Measure, like the gait
Of the Hopi. Dire foreknowledge, like the lightning

Zigzags of the Navajo blanket. Persistence,
Like the soft green and tufted sagebrush
Invisibly propagated out to the horizon.

Uproar of stars, or, here, *estrellas*, in the deep
Night of a piece with that night stretching up
From Mexico, night our unviolent conquistador,

His legions the stars speeding through space
At archangelic distances, no barriers
Withstanding, even at last the imagination,

Rooted as it must at first always be
In place and time, until these are swept aside
Before the onrush of what never began or ends.

XIV.

Late arrival at Flagstaff meant no room
To be found anywhere; until a last flophouse,
"The Pine Inn," admitted to having a bed —

Brass and "musical," it proved, as we climbed in
Under a bare bulb, the filament at lights-out
Triply reprinted on the dark. Stretches, whispers. . . .

Dawn. Dress, grub, then a sunwarm drive through forests,
Half gleefully, half grumblingly anticipating
The inexpressible geology of Grand Canyon.

(Here, I imagine, is the place to reconsider
An issue conceivably not laid to rest
Even by *The Prelude, Childe Harold,* or *The Bridge* —

That is, how much crosscountry observation
A poem can fairly admit. Next to fullness
Of feeling, mere recorded seeing should I view

As a negative, an absence, a gouging out
Accomplished by erosion under the headlong,
Superfluent wish to engrave in stone all

Fleeting colors, textures, and patterns of Nature,
All that is opaque to the imagination?
Description, though, goes deeper than a bleached-out Xerox,

Implicitly dispensing so much pleasure or pain.
And is "red" a color? Do wind-stirred pines "tremble"?
When images *Cover the World* like Williams' paint,

Their phrasing still manifests no loss of connotation
Or desire — which often acts simply to affirm
That earth, for some, is "apparel'd in celestial light.")

So for us that day, there at the origin
Of Bright Angel Trail: staggered, trying then also
To find words that would fall in love with what they saw.

XVI.

Cool sunlight on the rippling wheat-colored hills
Of the Bay environs. Buoyant recollections
Began to surface for you, anticipation

Based on two distinct epochs in your life, which
I struggled to apprehend with some echo of feeling
(Secretly abashed, however, at your having had

An existence before "us," the one now being confirmed).
Of your childhood, not much came back, even though
We passed your first house as we walked to the beach

For my long-deferred Pacific encounter — grandeur
At odds with the moderate combers washing up
On dirty sand among scraps of newsprint, bottles,

And dried kelp. At our backs, on the boardwalk,
A ramshackle funhouse broadcast grotesque
Tape-loop guffaws, farcical comment, one could feel,

On the Gold Rush. . . . Fog began to tumble in as if
To mute the sharp factual glare and make turning
Away from the moment easy as flagging down a taxi,

The driver briskly dispatched to Telegraph Hill,
Which ought to occupy the hour before dinner
With an overview, from Coit Tower, of the town plus

As many details as memory could add. Afterward,
We climbed down a vertical "street," wooden staircase
And landings overgrown with vines and scarlet fuchsia

Dripping silver beads in the mist-fine drizzle.
Houses perched intrepidly on the hillside, each
Linked to its neighbor by a few xylophone

Steps up or down, the pale white fog overlaid
On trees and gables like onionskin (on which
The dreamy child traces the outlines of "El Dorado").

XVII.

Wandering the Mission Churches, jolts of context
Put me in mind of Dante's tomb in San Francesco
At Ravenna. And of the jaunty flyweight friar,

Brother and rhapsodist to all creation,
The founder of poetry in Italian and forebear
Of a missionary effort active long after

These Californian outposts. Now his secular
Descendants, pilgrims of poverty, swarmed
All around — tonsure, no, but the patched motley

And outstretched palm of the mendicant (most
Working out of Haight-Ashbury, which had sunk
To normal pre-Love depression). Even Berkeley

Seemed chastened, half-deserted the day we spent
Visiting your former turf and friends still extant.
Revolution had subsided into health foods

And meditation, a reverent stillness suspended
Over all, the changed times no longer seeking change.
And rambles up through the hills almost despecified

One's sense of place as Everysky drew near
With clouds easily eternal in the worldwide blue. . . .
Which darkened, later, in the hotel window. Were we

Up for Chinese dinner? And a walk through North Beach
To Fisherman's Wharf (if only to prove you hadn't
Come home again. . . .) That much readier for tomorrow's

Glide through Golden Gate into Marin sunlight
And the road to Oregon (last lap through forests
Of giant redwood, which, with the bristlecone pines —

Methuselahs among the brother trees, in fact,
"The oldest living things on earth" — might stand
As a rare instance of the botanic sublime).

XX.

Portland. But less than ten days pass before
The road-seasoned pair pack up again and drive off
With your mother and Liza (a darker, smaller twin,

Hair parted in neat Indian style, hands stained
With print-maker's black or sepia) to spend two weeks
In a house at Arch Cape by the northern Pacific.

— Ocean that, real, took the measure of its myth,
Breakers toppling over like columns, brilliantly
Cold, onto long beaches of eggshell sand, the air

Mist-milky in daylight and clearing by evening,
When evergreens collected at the edge of the cliffs
To watch the sun ignite a skywide rose window

Before dropping into upheaval, anarchy,
Flamegold and midnight blue, the roiled unconscious,
Alien but exampling what the human includes.

Night brought the moon and a glow shed like silence
That danced among the rocks out to sea, on shoreward pines,
Tempting us from the screened porch down to the sand,

For ritual star census on the beach — vast galactic
Arch of spray, icy pinpricks less numberable
Than the aggregate mist above or sandgrains below:

Here, for any Einstein ready to think of falling
Upward into a boundless mist of light and time,
Was as much of wonder and terror as minds could know;

Until thought, vaporized by magnitude, burnt out
From keeping pace with the speed of light, pulled back
To earth, its spannable feet and minutes (where a body,

Warm, got by heart, accepts the gestures of formular
Protectiveness, shivering arm around slim waist,
As two turn and walk back to the lamplit house).

XXI.

Our hike through Ecola State Forest, the same
Tillamook Head that, sixteen decades before, a small
Whale-seeking party had climbed, then without the help

Of pendulum-swung paths up and up through Douglas
Fir, salal, hemlock, spruce, where now and again
We caught seablue vistas through screening branches.

Sweat drops. Mosquitoes. But by lunchtime we reached
An unvisited cove and settled on a natural table
In the craggy shadow of a cliff. Along with sandwiches,

Napa Valley pinot, and nectarines went the bonus
Of seeing you in your element, relaxed, tan,
Nicely filled out with summer-holiday flesh,

Hair streaming in the wind. . . . Like the comet, headlong
Through time, I can read it now, if then no similes
Proposed themselves — no more than the Valéryan truth

That, say, nectarines, to give pleasure, must be
Consumed; and likewise for these fleeting fair moments,
Which tell us to love the rose *because* it fades.

Mostly the sensation was of time to spare, to burn;
Even to read about the first troop withdrawals
From Vietnam, the long, dogged recessional

That would mount up year after year until, at last,
The ceasefire proclamation. Disasters, too, are mortal?
They have their conclusions, however incredible

To a generation for whom war had become
Axiomatic, an environ that had fostered and hardened
Habits of resistance not easily or soon

Put aside. Though a familiar love, under new skies,
Could lull them to sleep for days on end, drowning all
Grievances in the sea's millennial white music.

XXII.

Once in town again, I remember that, mornings,
I'd set myself to write. Small things at first. The "speech"
In still lifes, a vase holding a rainbow profusion

From your mother's garden, larkspur, daisies, cosmos
That *required someone to see and hear them, otherwise,*
What had been the point of flowering at all?

Not to respond in kind amounted to withholding
Fullness of being, casting them into outer darkness. . . .
However untutored my pen, still it meant to relay

The spark of life — transmitted here as once before
To the nerveless, upraised hand of Adam. No corner
Of the universe but a human impulse could warm it.

And I debated, that July, whether the moon herself
Felt the fledgling touch of emissaries Armstrong
And Aldrin, first to vault beyond the sphere of earth

And air to that bleak eyrie of glare and midnight
Cold, the prehistoric lunar dustscape. Its broadcast
Ghostly image sootblack and silver on our screen

Pierced deeply into unlikelihood, the twin
Astronauts in bulky diving attire clumsily
Planting a phosphorescent flag and sowing

Friday footprints, extrinsic trail markers wind
Nor rain for all of time would ever sweep away.
That night, at moonrise, I stepped outside to look

For changes in the broad, impartial face. No visible
Signs of gain or loss; but still some faintest sense
Of a new accessibility *and* a farther

Numerical remove now that consciousness
Had logged the entire mileage — its next task to beam
Back terse communiqués to tell us how things were.

XXV.

Summer slows down, gives notice of annual closure.
And we propose an end-of-season sendoff party —
Which might as well celebrate my birthday.

Someone suggests a theme; and why not *The Remembrance
Of Things Past?* Rôles grabbed or assigned — you
As Odette, Liza as Grandmère, old friend Gary

As Charlus, and me, feebly protesting, as Marcel.
Your mother, with gentle irony lost on no one,
Puts on a maid's cap and performs as Françoise.

Late August light out under beeches and hazels.
Odette in rose silk and a sable ostrich plume.
Charlus with diamond stickpin and moleskin gloves

That match Grandmère's powdered hair and eyebrows.
Françoise pours out linden tisane for a Marcel
Hardly paying heed — until he takes a madeleine

And, absently dipping it, tastes. The hand-held
Home-movie camera rolls and so do his eyes,
Shocked with remembrance. (An amazement staged and real:

For in fact I had drunk that infusion only
Twice before, in Avignon, and then in Paris.
From "farther than India or China" refracted tears

Stung the communicant the joke was on
As Rhone and Seine rose up and overflowed the banks
Of elapsed space-time, flooding through our tableau.)

Memory. A retrospective species of hope
Whereby one catches the habit of recalling
A future deep as fiction where *all will have been*

Well — the sparkling source with which we toast
Hazards undergone and weathered, the fugitive
Years at home finally in the immaterial.

XXVII.

Les vrais paradis sont les paradis qu'on a
Perdus — his meaning, I think, that he could be content
Only with what was *not there,* provided he found it

Again, this time a psychic essence within himself. . . .
My subject is our *union;* which was close even
At the conclusion — no less painful for all that

We used the term "amicable." For a long time
Separate paths had summoned us, a quiet past-tenseness
Already suffusing our sense of what our couple was,

When the moment came to make things formal.
The last two years passed reflexively, you now teaching,
Marking papers, meeting with your women's group,

I with no business anchor in the world, nothing
But a dutiful application to housework and
A passion for poetry based on few other warrants.

Then, having struggled to say the right farewells,
And not long after seen you snapped up by someone else
(Your new Victor, whom I judged suitable, as you did

My new Walter); having, by luck, mother wit,
Hard work, close scrapes, and the patient guidance of friends,
Come through, I can number myself among the fools

Who persisted in their folly — long enough
Now to recommend a less contrary approach to others
Thinking perhaps to venture something similar.

Yes, but advice. Would I have listened then? No more,
I guess, than those who crossed the Atlantic, forsaking
All, to rebuild Eden in waste wilderness;

No more than the captains told in advance what dangers
Faced them; or Dante, given a brief foretaste
Of his pilgrimage back to the lost Beatrice.

XXXI.

'We keep coming back here to each other,
And coming back for as long as we like.
A swallowtail poised above its iris,

Mars in peaceful conjunction with Venus,
The comet beaconed from the depths of space
To ride in highest heaven to the sun,

Its burning destiny and center, where
That light not changed by anything it shines
Upon brings home a life-lease of motion.

The master-light, the fountain light that sends
Its messenger with a live coal for me
To kiss, and be burned and forever set

Apart, on fire with purpose and a speech
Foreign almost to all but the nearest
Senses: rather than answer it I am

Answered, as this flooding certitude tells
Me and overflows so that the lowest
Object, least receptive impulse catches

Light and is permitted, altogether
Welcomed, loved, then gathered back at last
Into the slow diamond of the river

That first sent it forth. And what is
Earth but the shadow of another sphere?
We practiced our memories here and learned

To harvest a future not ruled by crops and years —
So much like this hillside grown up in grass,
With breeze-borne sun, fragrance of earth, of grass,

Of flowers, the rose-pink and white apple,
The white rush of a stream hidden nearby,
Love's new contentment changing forever.

The West Door

1988

The Band

Two, sometimes three come without being called.
Strictly breathing, down cool passageways
Where the hangings are (in silk cord,
Fable of the boar hunt) I go toward them.
Each one assumes a foregone expression.

(To have known the struggle'd turn literal
And still fathomed so deep, so free and dark?
I hadn't stopped to choose. But a cloudy voice
Spoke and reminded me that even a human
Face at point-blank range is a cyclops.)

They send me on, bathed in baptismal sweat
At the photographic daybreak —
Abdication more, it seemed, than dismissal.
My nearest chance was to be small, private,
Bold as a child. (Who, eyes lowered, keeps his counsel.)

Naskeag

Once a day the rocks, with little warning —
not much looked for even by the spruce
and fir ever at attention above —
fetch up on these tidal flats and bars.
Large, cratelike rocks, wrapped in kelp;
layer on imprinted layer,
umber to claret to olivegreen,
of scalloped marbling. . . .
Not far along the path of obstacles
and steppingstones considered,
fluid skeins of bladder wrack
lie tufted over the mussel shoals —
the seabed black as a shag's neck,
a half-acre coalfield, but alive.
Recklessly multiple, myriads compact,
the small airtight coffers (in chipped enamel)
are starred over with bonelike barnacles
that crackle and simmer throughout the trek,
gravel-crepitant underfoot.

Evening comes now not with the Evening
Star, but with a breathing fog.
And fog is the element here,
a new term, vast by indefinition,
a vagrant damping of the deep tones
of skies and bars and sea.
Sand, mud, sand, rock: one jagged pool
basining a water invisible
except as quick trembles
over algal weed — itself
half-absent, a virid gel.

Walking means to lose the way
in fog, the eye drawn out to a farther point,
a dark graph on the faint blue inlet watershine;
out to where a heron stands,
stationing its sharp silhouette
against the fogbright dusk.
Then, not to be approached,
lifts off and rows upward, *up, up,*
a flexible embracing-forward on the air,
rising out of view
behind an opaque expanse of calcium flame.

The great kelp-dripping rocks,
at random positions,
lost in thought and dematerializing
with the gray hour,
release, indelibly, their pent-up contents.
 — Even the scattered feathers here
are petrified, limewhite blades and stony down.
The sky, from eastward, deepens
with the dawning insight
as the seas begin to rise, the flats
slide away, the hulls bear off the ground,
and the eye alien to so self-sufficing
a tidal system turns and takes up how to
retrace the steps that brought it there.

The Candlelight Burglary

Open the vacation house after a winter's absence
And always some surface or hidden damage lies in wait —
Which goes to confirm the adage, still not obsolete,
That nothing really ever lasts but Time itself.
This year, it took the form of a second-story man;
Amateur, a detective also amateur would judge
From simple clues: a punched-in glass pane and (power
Was off) quick recourse to a candle-end, abandoned
On the mantel first by host and then by visitor —
This marble-pale wand, guttered, with a black wire
At its core. Wouldn't anyone have thought to bring
A flashlight? Well, a stand-in was near and apropos,
Provided by the absentee. "Through all her kingdoms,
Nature insures herself." True, and someone has to make
An inventory: *landscape with boy angling in rushing*
Stream; music system, more or less new; a chiming clock;
A Federal mirror. . . . Portable, negotiable,
They were what attracted his quick sleights of hand.
(At least the silver knew enough to stay in hiding.)
I'm sure this place was only one of several targets;
And then, effects not used nine months a year, we can
Obviously live without, hence may not have a right to. . . .

But look, now the hindered title, at one stroke,
Breaks free: mine — the law says so — if stolen from me.
(As losses help the gambler own up to what he lacks?)
In each drawer jerked open, a starry splash of marble,
Tears spilled over things taken, or rather those
Left behind for me to try to have and hold. . . . Imagine
The scene in eerie chiaroscuro that sprang into life
For that carpenter ant typing his way across the sill,

Who, how many nights ago, paused, antennae extended
At a blocklike grain of sugar, saw its quartz sparkle
In the glow and waver of invasive light, and then
A distant, crouching prowler, almost giant as his shadow.
A witness so marginal could hardly identify
Or think valuable what was spirited away
On the spread wings of cupidity-with-mind-made-up. . . .
Nor have followed the implications of a psyche's forcing
The issue, fear of discovery, of loss, the curious
Unconsidered spilling of light (and burning wax)
On all that's truly worth having. Worth having, that is,
When we keep, among other uninsurables, our word —
Goods possessed, for the most part, courtesy of darkness,
Which keeps things secret and doing so keeps them.

An Xmas Murder

He sits at the table, cloudlight of March
One tone with his hair, gray-silver on silver.
Midday fare in Vermont is basic enough.
In West Newbury, eggs and toast will do —
Though our doctor's had his sips of wine as well.
"Just don't be fooled. They're not as nice as you
Think they are. Live here a few more winters,
You'll get to know them clearer, and vice-versa."
Three years now, and we're still finding our way;
Newcomers need a guide to show them the ropes,
And he has been explaining township and county
Almost from the sunstruck day we met him
That very first July in this old house.
"I'll cite an instance of community
Spirit at work, North Country justice —
A case I just happened to be involved in.
No, please — all right, if you are having one."
He holds his glass aloft and then lets fall
A silence that has grown familiar to us
From other stories told on other days,
The will to recount building its head of steam.
"Well, now, you have to know about the victim.
His name was Charlie Deudon, no doubt Canuck
Stock some generations back, but he
Nor no one else could tell you — if they cared.
Deudons had been dirt farmers here as long
As anybody knew. They never starved
But never had a dime to spare, either.
Charlie resolved to change the Deudon luck.
And that's just what he did. Or almost did. . . .
He'd graduated two classes ahead of mine;

We knew each other, naturally, but not
On terms of friendship. Fact is, he had no friends,
And only one girlfriend, whom he married
Day after Commencement, June of '32.
And then he set to work and never stopped
Again, until they made him stop for good."
A wisp of a smile, half irony, half
Bereavement plays about his guileless face —
Red cheeks, blue eyes, a beardless Santa Claus;
Whose bag contains (apart from instruments
Of healing) stories, parables and proverbs,
Painkillers, too, for when all else fails.
"What kind of work had all that hard work been?"
"Oh, farming, like his elders, only better.
All the modern improvements, fancy feed
And fertilizers, plus machinery —
He was the first in these parts to milk
His herd in any way but as 'twas done
Since Adam's boys first broke ground with a plow.
And anything machines couldn't handle,
Charlie did himself, from dawn to midnight.
He never wasted a word or spilled a drop
Of milk or drank a drop of beer or liquor.
He was unnatural. *And* he made that farm
Into a showplace, a kind of 4-H model.
He made good money, yes, but not a dollar
Would he spend unnecessarily.
Do you get the picture? They hated him,
The boys that hung around the package store.
The most they ever got from tightfist Charlie
Deudon was a nod out from under his cap.
(His trademark — a baseball cap striped white and red.)
They envied him for getting his hay in first;
And there was more. A boy that he had hired,

By the name of Carroll Giddens, was their buddy.
Likeable fellow, regulation issue,
The sort that knocks back a pint or a fifth
In half a shake and tells off-color stories
Till he's got them choked to death with laughing.
'Course the wisecracks they loved best were those
About poor Charlie and his gold-plated farm. . . .
Just one more case of what's been often said
By commentators on democracy —
How it helps everyone keep modest."
Teasing mischief has crept into his voice.
A self-taught anthropologist as well
As teller of tales, he has other frames
Of reference to place around events
Local or international. He knows
That things can stand for more than what they are;
Indeed, says standing for things is why we're here,
And quotes chapter and verse to prove his point.
"Think of the worldwide scapegoat ritual.
In halfway civilized societies
An animal's the one relieved from life
Duty, am I right? A fellow tribesman
Will do in a pinch, if animals are lacking,
Or if communal fears get screwed too tight. . . .
Anyhow, it was clear that something more
Than common envy stirred up the lynch law.
Their own failure's what they wanted dead."
Seconds pass in silence as he stares
At something — perhaps a knothole in the pine
Floorboard. He looks up, eyebrows raised,
And twirls the glass stem between stubby fingers.
A coil of rope hung on the wall, we see,
Has made him pause and heave experienced sighs.
"Here. Have another. So: was Charlie punished?"

"I'm going to tell you — better me than others.
You see, I was involved — no, no, no,
Not in the deed, Lord, no, just as a witness.
It happened this way — hope you're not squeamish.
Charlie had this boy to help with chores,
The one named Carroll. Married, two kids, I think.
Not too reliable. But so few are;
Nor could you call his wages generous.
His buddies must have stood him drinks, is all
I can say. He'd a skinful half the time —
Was certainly drunk that Christmas Eve morning.
No reason to doubt what Charlie told his wife.
Charlie'd been up to help at six with the milking,
And Carroll, drunk as a fiddler's bitch, was there
Loading a pair of milk cans into the barrow.
He took a slip and the whole business spilled.
Wooden handle clipped him in the side,
And he fell, too, right in the puddle of milk.
And started *laughing.* Charlie, you can guess,
Didn't join in; he told him to get on home.
'What about the milk?' 'Go home,' he said,
'You're drunk.' 'But what about the milk?' asks Carroll.
'Comes out of next week's paycheck,' Charlie says.
And then the trouble starts, with Carroll swearing
And yelping, till Charlie gives him a little tap
And goes indoors. By then Carroll could tell
The barrow handle had cracked a rib or two.
He drove into town to see his doctor — that
Wasn't me — and word went out that Charlie
Had roughed up his innocent assistant.
That's all they needed, Carroll's friends. *About
Time that stuck-up bastard got his due,
He's gone too far this time, but we'll show him,*
Et cetera. . . . As it was Christmas Eve,

They had the leisure, the liquor, and the rope."
"They hanged him?" "No, that's not our way up here.
The honored custom's to dump them in the river.
You see, the river's New Hampshire all the way
Over to the Vermont side, and thus,
If the victim's still alive when he hits the water,
New Hampshire law enforcement and legal justice
Steps in. It tends to confuse the issue, see?
In wintertime, the river freezes over,
And you can't hope to fish the bodies out
Till the month of March at the earliest.
By then, who knows which state the victim died in?
A trick they've played a hundred years and more
Up in Woodsville, where the bridge is. That's where
The loggers used to go to spend their money
On booze and hookers — who'd arrange for them
To get knocked in the head at the right moment,
And pitched off the bridge into the water.
A famous local industry, but rather
Fallen on hard days by the early fifties,
Just like others more legitimate. . . .
Well, our local rowdies knew the routine,
And, when time came to follow up their threats,
They laid their plans according to tradition.
They knew that Charlie'd have to do the milking
Christmas morning same as every day.
And when he came into the barn to do it,
They'd be waiting for him. And that's what happened."

We strain forward to hear him tell the rest;
The narrative spell is on him, and on us.
His voice weaves through fine-tuned nuances,
With sudden leaps in volume and skittish phrases
That somehow help flesh out what he describes.

We see the sprawling barn across the highway
From the white-columned porch of the old house.
See the barn closed up tight against the cold,
And the blue-gray light of December dawn
As Charlie crosses the road to do his chores.
The roosters shriek their morning alarm, the big
Doors creak open on the darkness — a darkness
Slit with tight-strung wires of light knifing
Through cracks between the boards of the east wall.
Tufts of hay spill from cribs on both sides.
The waiting cattle stir and low as daylight
Breaks in on the darkness. Their master strides
In past the parked pickup truck, his pail,
A battered Rath Blackhawk lard can swinging
At his side, a whistled "Jingle Bells"
His fight song for the working holiday.
He hears the verses harnessed to his whistling,
The tune drawing its text along march tempo:
. . . *it is to ride in a one-horse open sleigh-ay!*
And then all changes. Smash of the blackjack
Against his skull, exploding carnival
Of fire-veined shock that flies to the far corners
Of night. Four assailants leap from the back
Of the truck and lift him partly erect, the quicker
To bind his arms behind and truss them to
His half-bent legs, as you might rope a steer
Or sheep you meant to brand or slaughter.
They take him out to where the car is waiting
And throw him in the trunk like a sack of feed.
Another car drives past but doesn't slow.
The bandits duck and climb inside their own.
Tires screech, the driver slams onto the highway,
A smile and wink all round as they drive north
To Woodsville. The sun is coming up when they

Reach the bridge and stop the car. The lid
Of the trunk's sprung open, its cargo discharged.
He is dragged to the railing, lifted, then heaved over.
The body falls, seeming almost to pause
In air before it hits the water and slides
Below the surface of the floating ice. . . .
Five miles back along the highway, the dark
Barn, the herd, a crushed tin pail, and signs
Of struggle in the dirt wait for someone's
Startled face, back-lit in the doorway,
To see them, then whip aside with a shout of terror.

"He wasn't found until spring thaw; he washed
Ashore just south of Bradford, still tied up
And looking like they'd tarred and feathered him —
Partly decomposed, but not his clothes.
First thing was an autopsy to test if he
Had died by drowning or was dead before
Going under. Conclusion was, he'd died
On land, so as I said, his death belonged
To the Green Mountain State's criminal justice."
"And what about the killers — were they caught?"
"Several suspects found themselves in jail —
And that's where I come in: as star witness.
It happened I was on the road that morning.
Real early. See . . . I'd promised my house guest
Of the night — young Marine on leave — I'd drive
Him back to Lebanon to grab his bus.
I always keep my word, especially
When given in the night hours. Nice boy —
He's been a good friend ever since. We'd said
Good-bye until the next three-day pass.
Well, I was driving home like Merry Christmas.
Into the headlights comes the Deudon farm:

And then I noticed the car. A two-toned Kaiser,
Side of the road, beneath a maple tree.
Didn't know whose it was or why it was there.
I saw one face, Calvin Renfrew's, that's all.
He didn't *have* wheels so far as I knew.
Occurred to me right then that something might
Be fishy; but locals never meddle till —
Till it's too late, sometimes. I should have stopped.
They might have banged me on the head, but then — .
Well, even as it is they got revenge.
I'm still alive, however, and mean to stay so."
He laughs a low laugh that would chill the devil . . .
Then takes up the thread — how when he heard the news
About Charlie's disappearance, he drove down
To tell the state trooper what he'd seen.
"That was the very next day after Christmas.
By nightfall Calvin Renfrew and Norbert Joiner,
The owner of the car (the Kaiser), and two
Associates were in custody. But not
For long. Someone bailed them out, someone
Rich, it had to be, an enemy
Or rival of Charlie's. That's often our way,
You know, to let others fix the person
We secretly hate, then give them secret help
When they get their paws burned in the process.
A lot of people coveted that farm,
However much disparaged it was in public.
When Charlie's widow put it up for auction,
Don't imagine nobody came to bid.
I still see things of his on others' farms.
What didn't surprise me either's how the town,
Lord help me, the whole county took the side
Of those arrested against the murdered man.
They said old Charlie had it coming to him,

Treating his employee that way. Meanwhile,
Carroll had quietly slipped across the border
To Canada; no way to prove that he'd
Hardly been hurt at all. So rumor flew.
If words could put you under ground, why Carroll
Was dead and buried six times over, a martyr
Hounded to his grave by a maniac
Who should have been taken care of years ago.
These are churchgoing people, too, but they
Figure they have a special insight as
To what the Boy Upstairs considers right.
Man is born for sorrow, so we're told,
And some try to make sure he gets a close
Acquaintance with the sorrow that's his due.
Meanwhile, if you can say the things people
Want to hear, then you may lynch at will."
He folds his hands and brings them to his chin.
"The rest of the story you can figure out
Yourself. Their lawyer asked the jury be
Directed by the judge to return a verdict
Of Not Guilty. Motion granted — as never
Before for a capital offense in *this* state.
They'd do it again, don't worry, if the case
Was dear to their concerns. Sounds cynical,
I grant you. . . . But then, you see, they started next
On me for fingering the guilty parties.
State trooper drops by to ask some questions.
Why was I on the highway that time of morning?
Oh? And who exactly was this friend?
Oh, really? Stayed the night, did he? I see. . . .
A doubt or two'd been raised before already,
Given that I had never married, *and*
Was locally famous for my special hobby.
I'm sure I've told you: I play a little pipe

Organ at church sometimes — I even travel
To play it elsewhere. I know organists
All over New England, and the town gazette
Used always to mention when I went to play
At musicales in other towns and states.
Nobody thought it mattered much beforehand,
But once the tale about the serviceman
Got out, my friends, well, you can just imagine.
Overnight young Dr. Stephens was
As 'musical' as you can be and not
Get tarred and feathered. My patients, some of them,
Began to melt away like ice cream. Stephens,
A local name, respected in these parts,
Became a byword for things we don't discuss.
I wondered whether I should move, of course;
Some rowdy threw a can of paint at the house;
I still get unsigned letters from time to time.
Things must be better where you two come from.
But this is where I've always lived, it's what
I know. If I had had the sense to pitch
Someone unpopular from off a bridge
Instead of enjoying music, chances are
I'd be a favorite son. In point of fact,
I've given up the organ, seldom play it
Nowadays. I've got a different hobby —
Your health, gentlemen! No more today, though.
Another call to make this afternoon.
But listen, now: if you'll come up to me
Next week, I'll play some pump organ for you.
I can still do a rousing 'Hornpipe' — the one
By Handel. Tourist attraction hereabouts.
I am fairly confident you won't
Ever have heard it played my way before."
He stands to go, consenting to be ushered

Out under the black trees of late March, down
To where his battered station wagon sits.
Thunder of engines takes him off. . . . But his words
Stay lodged in us like arrows, arrows aimed
As carefully as acupuncture and meant
Somehow to warn or counsel. Not that warnings
In the abstract often help stave off
Particular misfortunes, inevitably
The body of most stories drawn from life.
Misfortunes are the hinges life turns on?
Reprieves as well — along with persons, places,
Passions. A fluent paradox, the realm
Normally termed external, I mean its way
Of overhearing thought and mustering
Fresh evidence. . . . Today, for instance, how
New green on branches and a liquid birdcall
Suffice to announce the chaste approach of spring.

Assistances

Paris, London, Los Angeles —
men seated restlessly in a room
wait for clipped announcement of a name
grown faint and unfamiliar
to summon them upstairs.

The glare falling like cold enamel
on corked vials of venous blood,
each dyed with a message marked in code;
the dossiers that fatten
week by week, to whispered confidences
from white-clad figures in calm stances
conferring beyond the gauze of a curtain.

I think of you, friend and standard
bearer, first again to set out.
What can you not tell us about
the strong deliverance, the staggered
retreat of sound and sight,
loosing of the cord that bound
you to flesh, whose collapse still kept
a last function, the registry of pain?
Where yours ended, others take up
the relay, its sear and tremble at one
with hands that clasped, with hearts that leapt. . . .
silent injunctions made to those who wait,
balancing between patience and complaint,
until you softly call their name.

Welcome to Farewell

(Alaska)

At parallels high as these, invisible
circles, steadily more restrained,
catch last towns as they thin out
toward the Arctic vanishing point.

O perspective, give us scale
and depth, the touch to make a home
of temporary lodgings — doors opening
on new faces, the friendly lonely,
young and old,
whose year-round gazing straight up
at Polaris imparts a blue spin to their eyes;
whose voices, corrugated with magnetic North,
bark a discomposed welcome and gather us in.

Dublin, The Liberties

Summer, and low clouds hang over the Liberties,
over chimneypots and glistening slates
an echoing carillon of competing changes
rebounds against into attentive skies.

What part of the trouble that Guinness made
was channeled into Lord Iveagh's brick
developments, old benefactions lived in
but ignored or forgotten? Prehistoric
the sniff of burning turf,
an earnest against the drizzle's
brief, underemphatic
scrim that steams over broken walls
where snapdragons volunteer
a red or mustard salvo —
on occasion, the tender valerian,
as mauve as the Sacred Heart.

In shops along The Coombe
faceted crystal and silver candlesticks
wait for those who can find pleasure
in things still useful, things antique;
and houses, for their owners
off at work or gone for supplies —
the dog within dozing on his paws
near scattered envelopes
beneath the letter-drop.

Slender stair rail!
hold up your newel, a small white globe
poised to catch from landing windows

one pearled highlight, and another one:

This sphere makes no forecasts,
offers no hints for future tactics,
but draws into itself each muffled, metronomic
step heard passing on the pavement,
much as to take the pulse of time,
but time not quantified, the one-way push of fact.

Rainclouds shake down tribute
for the Liffey, goods of water
to be trundled gray-green past Wood
and Ormond Quay, the traffic
in opposite direction turning
up Bridge Street right into High,
into the Liberties and the late afternoon.
Driving will be an effortless flick
of horsemanship, deferring almost never
to pedestrians, paired or single, who
make for home (each green or blue door affixed
with a knocker clenched in the bronze
muzzle of a bearded lion).

Dublin 8's promissory brick
is what they know, they have declared for it.
The knocker growls or rattles
as the master of a six-room castle
(not counting cellar and attic)
opens his door to greetings from the dog
and bends down through a backache
to gather bills and letters, hearing the old
wind-up clock plucking its wide-spaced ticks —
plural but otherwise out of number —
from the shadows at the foot of the stairs.

Stephen Dedalus:
Self-Portrait as a Young Man

No. I will describe the arts of flying:
    First the surge, an indrawn sigh,
Familiar windiness of all
    The sunlit death-defying.

    Peak, now sink to hover —
Roads and plots; rivers, beds where they crawl;
    The stink of altitude zero
Propels me up past clouds for cover!

Father of Icarus, claim your right
    To carpenter and be no hero.
But some have shed lost wax sincerely, and I
    Chose the son, who chose flight.

New Year

Another year, another return —
Each one has drawn closer to home.
A perennial naif, whose pleased
intake of breath is meant to welcome
back the urban crush, prefers

familiar brickfronts and squares
even to vistas down the proud
colonnades and quays of Paris,
mountains lost among high clouds,
or domes at dawn in the pastel east.

These westward windows, fifteenth floor,
make a triptych frame for sunset —
which shows the buildings as somehow more
thoughtful than they often get
described as being; while the sky,

with blue impartiality,
may be forecasting the first
snowfall. . . . To sense purpose in turning
to the desk again seems right,
the crossed-out sentences and lines

summoning words and pauses always
nearer those that will be felt
as having stood by from the start,
waiting to assume their place.
The heat clicks on. Somewhere a bell. . . .

All the objects here have twinned themselves

with stories. The room's a cradle, or an ark;
it says that half the point of our departure
is coming back — suggestion followed by one
who breaks off work to watch the setting sun.

FROM

Autobiographies

1992

A Village Walk Under Snow

Roiling flakes,
The lunge of a million carousels
In free fall makes
Frame houses' old pastels

By contrast bright
As fresh enamel; while that Ford
(In negative white)
Reveals the silkenly scored

Streamlines wind
Tunnels were designed to test.
Cold weather, friend,
Truest if not the best,

Is seeing saving —
This tufted pine branch, thick with spume
As a poised shaving
Brush or egret's plume,

Mine to keep?
And those post-Xmas Xmas trees
Fallen asleep
In snow and left to freeze

On kelp-strewn sands of
The vacant public beach. . . . Enough
That wheeling bands of
Gulls patrol a rough-

Hewn, bile-dark sea,
Rising to meet the falling sky
Where gulls are free,
Hovering, to dive or cry.

(A bold one dives
Right now, just past my head — one more
Of those close shaves
Outdoors is noted for.)

Jumbo lace,
A complex tire-track hems the path
My steps retrace
In the homeward aftermath —

Gray skies, bare trees,
Houses seen through veils of snow,
Affording ease
Good for an hour or so.

Cannot Be a Tourist

Not casually. Within two days
Streets and vista are mine forever,
Some last few wisps of jet lag clearing
As senses expand to occupy
A space already second nature.

How many facts, though, work against
Staying put. A rented house;
An unknown language stumbled over;
Formal obligations, debts,
In taut suspense back where we vote.

Brought home so often, still the dried
Pages of the journal are more
Compelling than they have a right,
Much reasonable right, to be.
Only alight on them and now

Ancestor olives near Delphi
Stand in an oddly youthful trance;
The vines outside Siena, leaf
By jagged, gold-veined, classic leaf,
Outline the sun in a dust of earth;

Bronze, coal-green, the Haitian bantam
Stalks a wall spilled over with red
Bougainvillea; or Quai Voltaire's
Streaked pediment enshrines a crush
Of half-nude marble, artist-cohorts

Living it up in their garret (the Seine

By night, each lamp secreted in oyster
Mist). . . . Facts be damned: some part follows
Hereafter and continues. At home
Where the heart enlarged by affection is,

Whoever could not be a tourist
Shuts the door pro forma only —
Aware, even so, that form's good practice
For firm conclusions, holding steady
When time says, "Bid the earth farewell."

My Neighbor, the Distinguished Count

At first thinking it was harmless
Enough, I told myself I had pints
To spare, so why refuse a simple favor?
Hannah could have turned him away at the door,
But I didn't think that was necessary.
I'd always liked his mother and father
(Whom he grew sadly to resemble less
As months passed, his condition progressing).
The visits came bearably seldom,
And no one could have brought everything
Off more smoothly. Afterwards I'd feel calmer,
Drowsy, reconciled. Easy to see why
People once regularly bled themselves
For medical reasons, though of course
That was a cure normally reserved for men,
Who labor under greater pressures than we.
Easy, too, for one to think of donor service
As the good deed for the day — thy neighbor
As thyself, no? — a neighbor so visibly
In need, his pale brow furrowed, an electric
Tic active at the corner of the mouth.
Thoughts less reassuring surfaced later
When what he meant as compensation arrived,
The flowers, touring car idling outside,
Heart-shaped boxes of intricate chocolates,
Young Burgundies, spring lamb nicely done up.

Why did the visits multiply? No doubt
There had been other clients beforehand,
But perhaps they moved or died, who can say?
Or else he'd concluded I was, for the moment,

A likely vintage and a pleasant temperature.
One afternoon I brought myself to ask.
"I come to you, dearest, because you think
Of me. An irresistible summons."
Manners: how tell an acquaintance serene
In the conviction of having been your constant
Preoccupation for how long now that,
In fact, you hardly ever thought of him?
Chided jokingly, could he read minds?
He answered, even better than that, he could read
Signs. It seemed I'd left them everywhere.
And true messages always reached their addressee,
Wasn't it so? From this I knew the mere facts
Of our erratic situation counted for nothing
When placed beside his own inner persuasions.

He told me he'd been seeing more "signs" than ever,
And certainly he came to me more and more often,
Insisting I call him Tony, as his friends did.
I tactfully refused. When dealing with
Obsession, as a rule the safest plan
Is to maintain a strict formality.
Yet it occurred to me at some point symptoms
Might creep up with no warning. You would be
Quite unaware of new expressive habits
Connected, *he* said, to your daydreams — which,
In this case, were also traps. I must outwit them.
Have you ever tried *not* to think of a face
Or a voice, going over each confused tangle
On the mental loom to make sure the banned
Thread of reference doesn't appear in it?
How often I longed to stay profoundly asleep
And never be conscious again. . . . Waking,
I brooded on little but how to stop our meetings,

A rebellion no doubt proving just how much his
I was. For what demonstrates more clearly
The power of a creator than fierce resistance
From his creature? If alive, it will be free.
Free, it will insist on its own ideas —
And so, at last, have to be disciplined.

Lately, there's been another turn of the screw.
His chauffeur arrives with a silver cover
Under which lies a rat, spitted and roasted.
Or his gardener will leave a fistful of poison ivy
Tied with catgut in the mailbox. And then, the dresses,
Too small, too large, jaundice yellow, black violet.
Now, it's hopeless, no hour passes without thoughts
I've given up trying to sidestep or quench —
Which he has taken as license to appear
At all hours, day or night, and send, with thanks,
More frequent tokens of declining esteem.
I gather from what he says (we sit, we chat)
I'm not what I used to be, his visits, indeed,
A gesture of sentimental gallantry.
Apparently there's someone else less . . . shopworn.
Yesterday I asked, in a voice admittedly weak
(The constant drain), *why* he still bothered to call.
"Because, my dear, you haven't stopped thinking of me."
I blushed (faintly), he smiled, and when he left there was —
Where? Oh yes, the kitchen — a coiled blood sausage,
Old, wizened, utterly dried out, resting
On a small hand mirror. I remember this now
Only because I can't help doing so, aware
Of the acrid little joke: that, according
To his iron code of gamesmanship, I have
Just authorized another courtesy call.
In full knowledge also (hideous necklace of sores

That no longer heal, veins like blackened vines!)
That today he will come for the last time.
My quaint request is that the coup de grâce
Be administered by himself alone and not
By any of his troop of haggard followers
Who have begun to congregate outside.
Thick as autumn leaves ready for the bonfire,
They throng my doorstep, basset eyes pleading;
And, without giving their names, pronounce my own,
A silken cajolery drolly intoned, as if —
As if they were old friends I'm about to rejoin.
And then, this driving pain in my eyeteeth,
This thirst. . . . Well, you see, I want my turn, too.
A country mile off, I saw and felt the change.
It has the magnetism of all dimly grasped ideals.
Surely by now no one can say I am not deserving?
I understand the problems and am willing to work.

Look, he has arrived. Hannah's white cap vanishes
Down the dark passage and is replaced by his face
Floating in the gloom like a full moon, eyes lowered,
His left hand dangling a gold watch on its long chain.
Never have I seen so much, nor ever felt so deeply —
Hence the sudden piercing intimation of what I am
One day to be, this twilit picture of discretion, the set
Of his features calm as an engraving of one who lets words
Of gratitude pass in silence as he settles to the task.

Contemporary Culture and the Letter "K"

First inroads were made in our 19-aughts
(Foreshadowed during the last century by nothing
More central than "Kubla Khan," Kipling, Greek
Letter societies, including the grotesque KKK —
Plus the kiwi, koala, and kookaburra from Down Under)
When certain women applied to their moist eyelids
A substance pronounced *coal* but spelled *kohl,*
Much of the effect captured on Kodak film
With results on and off camera now notorious.
They were followed and sometimes chased by a platoon
Of helmeted cutups styled the *Keystone Kops,* who'd
Freeze in the balletic pose of the letter itself,
Left arm on hip, leg pointed back at an angle,
Waiting under klieg lights next a worried kiosk
To put the kibosh on Knickerbocker misbehavior.
Long gone, they couldn't help when that hirsute royal
King Kong arrived to make a desperate last stand,
Clinging from the Empire State, swatting at biplanes,
Fay Wray fainting away in his leathern palm
As in the grip of African might. Next, marketing
Stepped up with menthol tobacco and the brand name
Kool, smoked presumably by models and archetypes
Superior in every way to Jukes and Kallikaks.
By then the race was on, if only because
Of German *Kultur*'s increasing newsworthiness
On the international front. The nation that had canned
Its Kaiser went on to sponsor debuts for the hero
Of *Mein Kampf,* Wotan of his day, launching thunderbolts
And Stukas, along with a new social order astonishing
In its industrial efficiency. His annexing
Of Bohemia cannot have been spurred by reflecting

That after all Prague had sheltered the creator
And in some sense alter-ego of Josef K.,
Whose trial remained a local fact until the fall
Of the Empire of a Thousand Years, unheard of in "Amerika"
Of the Jazz Age. But musicians Bix Beiderbecke and Duke
Ellington somehow always took care to include the token
Grapheme in their names, for which precaution fans
Of certain priceless '78s can only be grateful.
They skipped and rippled through a long post-war glow
Still luminous in the memory of whoever recalls
Krazy Kat, Kleenex, Deborah Kerr, Korea, Kool-Aid,
And Jack Kennedy. Small wonder if New York had
A special feeling for the theme, considering radical
Innovations of De Kooning, Kline, and Rothko. This last
Can remind us that bearers of the letter often suffered
Bereavement and despair (cf. Chester Kallman) and even,
As with Weldon Kees, self-slaying. Impossible not to see
Symptoms of a malaise more widespread still in a culture
That collects kitsch and Krugerrands, with a just-kids lifestyle
Whose central shrine is the shopping mall — K-Mart, hail to thee!
To "Kuntry Kitchen," "Kanine Kennels," and a host of other
Kreative misspellings kreeping through the korpus
Of kontemporary lingo like an illness someone someday
(The trespass of metaphor) is going to spell "kancer."

True, there have been recidivists in opposite
Direction (a falling away perhaps from the Platonic ideal
Of tò kalón*) like "calisthenics" and Maria Callas,
Who seem to have preferred the less marblelike romance
Of traditional English. This and related factors make all
Supporters of the letter "k" in legitimate forms
And avatars cherish it with fiery intensity —
All the more when besieged by forces beyond
Anyone's control, at least, with social or medical

* tò kalón: Greek, "the beautiful"

Remedies now available. Dr. Kaposi named it,
That sarcoma earmarking a mortal syndrome thus far
Incurable and spreading overland like acid rain.
A sense of helplessness is not in the repertory
Of our national consciousness, we have no aptitude
For standing by as chill winds rise, the shadows gather,
And gray light glides into the room where a seated figure
Has taken up his post by the window, facing away from us,
No longer bothering to speak, his mind at one with whatever
Is beyond the ordinary spell of language, whatever dreams us
Into that placeless place, its nearest image a cloudless
Sky at dusk, just before the slow ascent of the moon.

La Madeleine

1.

Posters of Juliette Greco, the Eiffel
Tower. A good French bistro in the Village,
Its cuisine by some oversight not yet
Widely known; all the more murmured over
By our party of four avid diners,
Leaning forward over the red-checked cloth.
First course dispatched in record time, I could
Be more deliberate with the second,
Enough to admire each tender forkful
Of the fragrant *Coquille St. Jacques,* steaming
In its ribbed scallop shell — eyes even so
Straying to glance at plates on either side.
In fact, we all sampled each other's entrée
And, satisfied, returned to our first choice.
When time came to moan at the dessert list,
Among the dazzlements our friend Richard,
The translator of Proust, saw handwritten
Copperplate flourishes near the bottom
Propose "Compote de Fraises avec Madeleines."
In lieu of some duller, full-dress homage,
We had them brought for all of us, berries
In red syrup, plus moist, butter-and-egg
Cakes, fluted backs golden by candlelight.
Why *don't* they call these little scallop shells
"Les biscuits St. Jacques"? No, another more
Romantic saint has given them her name.
(Mary Magdalene's the revered object
Of pilgrimages as well, her grotto
In Provence — but let's postpone that visit.)

My story over coffee
Began with a concert given at La Madeleine,
The church disguised as a svelte Greek temple,
Where Parisians rich or devout or both at once
Come to see and be seen or, who knows, seek
Forgiveness for sins like self-righteousness.
Still queasy from a three-hour lunch, never mind,
I'd bought my ticket, let music be the tonic
For day-of-arrival hyperactivity. . . .
Ushers were all women of the congregation,
Older, *soignées*, managing subtly to convey
The impression that each was the finer, calmer
Outcome of a worldly personal history now
Put aside in favor of good works and some ideal
Of repose. The one who seated me, gray silk jacket
Over pleated mauve *charmeuse*, smiled and gravely
Searched my eyes as I did hers, both of us refreshed,
I think, poised at ready for an hour of colliding
Gold reverberations, courtesy of Gabrieli. . . .
A week later in a ward of the American Hospital
I saw that same devout double of Jeanne Moreau
Making what looked like a round of volunteer
Visits to the dying — one of them a friend
I'd come to see. The image surviving, framed
Against starched white bedclothes, is a dark profile
Bent slightly forward as she takes the elderly,
Mottled hand of a patient, his health now broken,
Yet only a year ago young and strong and immune.

2.

Proust would have been a flâneur in La Madeleine,
Along with how many prototypes of Odette de Crécy.
And what did he know about its patroness?

A few paintings from the Louvre or Venice,
Namesake heroines in Balzac and Fromentin,
Plus his own in the story *L'Indifférent*. . . . I
Remember from a visit to Galilee (four years
Now) on our drive north along the bluegreen lake,
A signpost marked MIGDAL (in Hebrew: "tower").
That must have been, seventy generations back,
The place of origin of Saint Mary, Jesus' friend,
The only woman that might count as a disciple
And first to recognize, according to Saint John,
Her risen Lord. Whether as well the suppliant
Who wept at Jesus' feet and dried them with her hair,
Sumptuous, "a great sinner," with gold to spend
For an alabaster vase of fragrant spikenard —
Well, tradition's the richer for having thought so.
Because of their devotion, Mary of Magdala
And the Beloved Disciple in time emerged
As closest to his heart — with iconic appeal as well,
To judge by Renaissance art and its aftermath.
"Let him who is without sin cast the first stone at her."
Weakness of the flesh was routine, so decreed
The late Church fathers as the taxonomy
Of transgression was being drafted. Witness
Paolo and Francesca, lovers whose misdeed
Weighed just enough to earn them a fiery nest
At the whirlwind's heart in upper Inferno —
And perpetual fame in the Testament of Beauty.

3.

You were one of those four at dinner, remember?
Any candlelit meal by extension also serves
To celebrate years of settled union. The lens
Of the mind's eye is I guess appropriately

Vaselined by time so that scenes from the life
Return in a tender, peach-toned soft-focus.
Happy years? Yes, at first. Afterwards, four or five
Spent *together* at least, trying to remember
Happiness is only one kind of fulfillment.
A riddle to imagine how you see us now —
But then, I never knew, not even in the early days,
Before you came to see larks and sparks (Parents,
Avoid them) as betrayal pure and simple.
Thinking of you intent on *Pelléas* (Act III:
Mélisande leans from a tower window and lets
Yards of golden hair cascade over her lover),
Your right hand aloft and darting, to assist
The maestro; or tickled by a page in Colette;
Or quoting an Auden line that seemed to hold
All wisdom, who wouldn't assume words and music
Had some point for you in mere experience,
Were more than self-enclosed palaces of art,
In fact, offered shelter and counsel even to us
With our grouches, gourmandise, and dirty socks?
No? On conduct taken for granted in Bloomsbury
Or Montmartre down came a gavel termed *Love.*
The daze of seeing you doubt I did, the jolt
Of hearing instinct or impulse interpreted
As callousness aforethought — one more lesson
In the power of words, nothing like clock hands
Unfailingly recycled to the harmless
Hour before what was said was said. . . . Two years along,
I can see, though, that time is absolution, and many
Rehearsals have now sublimed the old debate
Into light breezes like those the opera chorus
Irresistibly wafted into the key of F major,
Or like a barcarolle, a waltz, a cradle song —
"Lay your sleeping head, my love, human. . . ."

4.

Faceless harm, invasions up from the id,
That underworld mined with caverns accessible
Only through the Gate of Horn, or the maudlin
Inarticulation that overflows censorship
When we stretch out for today's analysis
In the position of love and sleep and death.
Where does the violence come from, and who
Is being killed. . . . The undeterred cast a stone,
And another and another, heaping a rubble cairn
Over the buried victim's blood-soaked clothes,
That fossilized taboos, appearances, the will
Of the majority, this time also be enforced.

5.

Those travels in the provinces,
Up mountain to Vézelay;
Or underground in Lascaux
To trace vestiges left
By a social unit clothed
In half-cured pelts of a mammal
Cousin at many removes,
First effort to draw a fine
Distinction between the human
And the animal. Outlines
Of aurochs, stag, and ibex
In soot or manganese
Dredge up iconic imprints
Of internal prehistory —
Attraction and disgust
At the touch of a furred flank,
Perceived at once as foe

And bloodhot, maternal
Source of nourishment.
Would the stag at last forgive us
For bringing him down with a spear,
And send us more of his kind
In seasons to come? Only
If we kept his image alive
In a vault deep underground,
Where he ranged for humid aeons
Among four-legged fellows
At ease in the limestone fields
Enclosing a pitch darkness
Now and then broken when swaying
Torchlights rounded a veer
In the cave (distant, inverse
Forebear of the highrise),
Like a long chain of molten
Gold, to bring new cravings,
Forms, propitiations,
To hallowed flocks already
Portrayed by an earlier art,
Memorial of what's called
(After the cave's first name)
The Magdalenian culture.

A pause here before I forget
(Sympathy for the waiter
With several plates on his arm)
To mention Sainte-Baume, Mary's
Hermitage late in life.
Golden Legend recounts
How with Martha and Lazarus
She sailed to Gaul, arriving
At Roman Marsilia,

Where (the spirit's wings
Widespread) she preached in *koinē*
To listening multitudes
Of stolid barbarians —
And, years after, withdrew
To a hillside cave near Aix,
Her final days told out
In prayerful penitence,
Itself the fragrant balm
Preparing her body for death.
Today's visitor enters
A humid darkness, the rough
Stone floor cratered with puddles
Reflecting liquid shards
Of larkspur blue and scarlet
From stained-glass ogive windows.

In cool silence you may
Say a prayer to the saint,
Rise and find a path
Through trembling, jewel-like water,
Pause at the door to look back —
Then exit into the whitehot
Sun towering over the Midi.

6.   *Feast of St. James, 1989*

Dear David, Happy fifty-sixth birthday. Shall I
This time write (as I daily think of you)
And allow friendship to go on evolving —
In some ways more evenhanded than back
When you were with us, subject to wincing
Stresses the temple of the body has to bear,
Hunger pangs, noise, fatigue, bronchitis.

The week of your death, along Village sidewalks
Linden flowers dusted the air with the faint
Potpourri that will now always summon up,
In bouts of silent thought, our own *belle époque.* . . .

At any dinner party the best finale was you,
A compote of phrases derived from native wit
And close readings of the Elizabethans,
James, Yeats, Stevens, and *The Remembrance.*
Involuntary allusion smiles and sees you
As a second Charles Swann, relaxed and upright
In a *traghetto* as you skimmed across the Canal
Under the shadow of Santa Maria della Salute
To lend some luster to a gathering where,
Apparently, simply leaning against a door,
Arms folded, face lit by an amused, benign
Expression, could magnetize them to your side,
Eager for smiling urbanity's angle on whatever
Venice might be buzzing about that given day.
You had (outside *Swan Lake*) no single Odette,
Rather, a series, cygnet after black or white
Cygnet, whom with a twinkle you brought to parties
(Depending) or skipped parties to stay home with. . . .
Memory's parenthetical invasions of the daily
Round promise to keep you now and future decades
The faithful companion of my "decrepit age,"
As Yeats ("The Tower") called the rest of his climb.

Venice from time immemorial beset by plagues,
No surprise should the palazzo's proprietress,
Hearing of your condition, panic and with all
The innocence of misinformation have your floor
Fumigated, clouds of tear-gas mingling with those
In the library ceiling's frescoes. . . . When you turned

For a last look at the Barbaro (before the long
"Wreck of body, slow decay of blood"), slimegreen
Waves at work to dissolve how many surrounding
Morose or fanciful façades, over the Mahlerian rush
Of waters and motors, bells tolling from the distant
Campanile, dialect outcries, adagio strings
Wafting across the Canal, was there also, if heard
Only in the inner ear, a faintly beating sibilance,
Descending, settling to rest, the wings of the dove?

7.   *LA MADDALENA*

The baroque streetwalker Caravaggio painted,
His contemporary, a piece of cake from Trastevere
In Fortuny brocade, slumped in a chair next cast-off
Finery, serpentine chains of massive gold,
A broken string of pearls, vial of fragrant oil
She can no longer pour over the Master's head
And anoint him king. Head bowed, auburn hair
Streaming over her shoulders, behold a type
Of the unfaithful, returned from the fleshpots,
Agonized and with no intimation that dawning
Day in a garden outside the city will find her
Weeping by the tomb ("Elle a pleuré comme
Une Madeleine," as older women used to say),
Only to hear her name and answer, "Rabboni!"
Then be commanded to go and tell the brothers,
Her "I have seen the Lord!" echoing down
Twenty centuries in the breaking of the bread —
Whenever broken "for the remembrance of me."

8.   *Feast of St. Mary Magdalene, 1990*

Mary of Magdala,
Vividest apostle,
Teach me to be faithful;

And to discount mistakes
Others may have made
Out of pain and confusion.

Pray for the sick, the dying,
And those who watch at their side.
Help us to dry our tears;

Or, if they will not cease,
Then let them bathe the feet
Of our best advocate.

At each new step of the stair,
Blessed Mary, pray for us —
And remember us on that day.

The Jaunt

In party outfits, two by two or one by one
(I was expected to go along as well),
They step up the steep gangplank, hands on
Metal railing. The river, youthful also
In midnight blue with sunset-tinted wavelets,
Lets them borrow its broad back
For an evening's unhurried round trip,
Which won't interrupt old river habits for long.
Not the chop and churn of big propellers
As the rocking stern heaves off and wheels fanwise
Into the current, nor a short blast from the stack,
Not the up-tempo drumbeat of the black-tie combo
Nor an answering fusillade of popped corks, not geysers
Of laughter pitched flagpole high among flailing
Limbs out on the polished floor nor the mixed
Babble of sideline comment over bubbling glasses
Can shake that seamless imperturbability. . . .

When the springy net of sparkles has shrunk and faded
Out of sight, the last rough throb been coaxed
From the tenor sax's frog-in-the-throat, the final
Needling tremolo of the clarinet been wrapped up
In distance, suddenly it is strange to be here
In lilac afterglow with trout-leap and mayfly. . . .
Strange, too, how our part of the river continues
To trundle along its tonnages of water and motion.

The unused ticket spins to the ground.
As much as any person not two people can
I miss the jaunt, for just this one hour of dusk. . . .
Then, a veiled echo, my name called as I turn

To answer, eyes adjusting to where we are
At the pivot of night, the cusp of light.
Light enough to feel our way back to the grove
Of alders along the curving path beside the river;
Light enough to recognize my life when I see it,
Going in its direction, more or less at the same pace.

From 1992

for Christopher Corwin

1.

1949

I took the water she gave me, a dark young woman
in a "Spanish," off the shoulder, ruffled blouse —
a cover girl, almost (like the maiden on the Sun-
Maid raisin box), remembering to smile for tourist
cameras, a bright "wine-stain" birthmark
on her arm prominent as she calmly
ladled draughts from *The Fountain of Youth*
into a paper cup, whose contents ignited
in noonday light. This was St. Augustine,
Florida, summer I was six going on seven.
Too young to see the paradox, I drank; and waited
for legendary water to transform my life.

The town boasted its fort from the Golden Century,
turreted, built of tabby, and "the oldest schoolhouse
in the United States." A steady stream of visitors
kept things lively, half to see the monuments, half
to turn a tone darker; and there was always
the barely reined-in surge of tropic leaves and flowers.
Ponce de León's public-relations name for the land
had in a sense come true, and these middle-aged
vacationers rediscovering their bodies
found a source mazes of cypress swamp
and jaws of the dragon had kept from him.

(I'll say our server was Dolores Curtis,
a Tampa native, 23. Day's work done,
she walks to her apartment, a new Spanish

mission stucco, tiled in red terracotta.
The small white Zenith radio crackles
a broadcast speech of Harry Truman's.
Station break, static, a cigarette ad,
followed by Glenn Miller. Off comes the peasant
costume, panties, bra; on comes the shower.
A String of Pearls. . . . Bright drops spill
on white, honeycomb-patterned tiles
as she swaddles the towel into a turban,
pink hibiscus nodding outside the window,
the blood-red stamens dusted gold with pollen.

By 6:30 Wayne's driven up in his green Packard.
A "shave-and-a-haircut" knock on the door. "Two bits,"
she says as she lets in his 100-watt smile,
fending him off, a little. Where to? The Shangri-La
Drive-In, famous for shrimp, fries, and Schlitz.

Afterwards they drive to the beach and park.
Lucky Tiger tonic slicking his pompadour
in place fails to hold as he takes a movie pose
over her. August heat and damp, a single mosquito
keening around them. She lets him go just so
far, not a step more until they're married.
Wayne works for his daddy, owner of five hundred
acres of citrus out from East Palatka, plus
some swamp acquired during the Florida Bubble.
He's supposed to make his own way, though,
and hasn't saved enough for down payment
on a house, not yet. A deep kiss, and it's too
far, as waves crash and collapse, foam races
along the shore, salt fragrance, the fountain of youth.)

My first journey anywhere. Ragged silhouette

of distant palms, percussive sun, and,
farther out, beach grass and low shrubs that dot
the rolling dunes, dimpled swells of sand gliding
down to the brushed cymbals of an old Atlantic
whose unhindered horizon and somersaulting waves
left me dazed, thirsty, and blinking. The sunstarred
heft of the tide built and rebuilt its seagreen
redundant thunderheads to the steady roar
and quick applause of invisible crowds. A sand
castle modeled on their Spanish prototype
took form at the edge as I patted grainy
mortar into place and shaped a turret, only
to have it erased, along with my childishly
scrawled name, while the *perpetuum mobile*
waves slung their white lassoes higher and higher. . . .

All of this as we half-orphans put out tendrils
toward our new mother, twelve years Daddy's junior.
Herself a World War widow at 25, she was "brunette,"
stylish, affectionate, and liked to laugh.
Youngest of the children and the first,
in trustful desperation, to call her "Mama,"
I knew already *something* was wrong with me.
Missing a scented, nervous warmth since my second birthday,
I was fearful of everything — of transgression
and the punishment that followed, of going
to unfamiliar places, meeting strangers there.
Even now I dread these unmasked statements,
their therapeutic slant and trust in fact,
failure to scan or use productive rhyme
or metaphor. Yet can't deny the will to
set out in search of what it is that shaped
one witness's imagining of time
(five late-20th century decades sifting

numbered moments through the infinity
sign's tipped hourglass) and make available
the content of the world that is my case —
composed in part by all those I have met,
thinking through the story of who we are.

2.
1971

"C.C. Rider, see what you have done . . ." came over
the car radio from some station west of Twin Falls,
Idaho, where Ann and I'd quarreled through a restless
night in early June, in fact, had been on edge
half the drive through Wyoming (travel's downside
tendency to fray good humor). Here we were
on the road again, to spend a second summer
with her mother in Oregon, a chance to look
closer at things a first encounter only part-way
comprehended. . . . And last night? A few too many
shots on the rocks, one delayed result,
that driving felt queasy as the Rambler
hugged hairpin curves of a state highway roughly
paralleling whitewater rapids of the Snake.
A quick sarcasm, and we picked up (eagerly?)
the argument where midnight had left it.
Car and wheel close to blind rage, for safety's
sake I pulled off the road, fifteen miles
south of Boise. Unbroken expanse of pale
blue sky; far pastures; leaning fencepost
overgrown with wild sweetpea, the summer bees'
resort. Attention bent to that particular
fragrant hum, which I stabbingly
perceived as a nectared résumé of our best
moments. "Do we call it off then?" Anyone

could tell more was meant than the quarrel,
or why so loud a heartbeat in my ears?
Once-in-a-lifetime glances exchanged.
Solemn nod, blinking eyes. Then an hour of silence.
Almost to the day, one slowly grinding year
later, sharp legal instruments set us apart. . . .

How much plot unfolds on our highways,
the routine vehicular habit, cradle to grave
In Conestoga style, self-contained movable
houses like the small silver one we saw
sail past us that morning, a single driver
at the wheel of the Chevy hauling it.

(He wondered who they were, those two parked
roadside out there in the lap of nowhere.
Mike Kovich, 36, of The Dalles, Oregon,
on the loose and in transit after the splitup.
Connie — his ex — got the house but told him
to keep his stupid trailer. She plans to stay
in Salt Lake City, on 9th Street, a view
of the Wasatch Mountains to the east and, opposite,
the Angel Moroni atop the Temple spire. In time,
of course, you stop seeing any view. Her job
with Prudential takes up the daylight hours,
besides which, she has a little girl to raise.

When Mike told her he was leaving, she cried —
more for Amber's having to grow up without a father
than anything else. He wanted her to break the news.
Amber was already down with a cold, and it just
seemed really mean. She saw red and realized
she'd clobber anyone who tried to hurt her child,
then thought, Wait, this is how people go off
the deep end. Mike hadn't been himself a couple

of years now, he missed his buddies back
in The Dalles. A lot of Vietnam vets are moody,
it said in *Family Circle*. He wouldn't even
watch TV with her, just sat in the den and fiddled
with his rod and tackle or read through beatup
back issues of *Field and Stream*.
They'd stopped making love, naturally, and some
nights Mike would get in late, smelling of booze.
OK, he didn't like his job with the power company,
but why take it out on her? She's embarrassed
at being a divorcée, and just might remarry if
somebody decent who doesn't mind she's already
got a kid shows up and asks her the right way.
But like, she's nothing special, really. It would
take a bighearted kind of guy even to notice her,
and frankly there just aren't that many around.

Mike feels bad about leaving and knows he has
hurt his little daughter. If he had it to do
over again, maybe he'd have stayed and given
the hell up like everybody else. Just that,
nighttimes, when you wake up and begin to see
white water shunting over the rocks, a tall stand
of Engelmann spruce above. . . . You cast and recast,
the little speckled fly dancing from wavecrest
to crest, Jay (who'd been their best man) fifty
yards upriver, likewise, in a different rhythm.
Six-packs nest in the cooler, a hawk balances
on an updraft, the air-conditioning pouring out
of the woods is a green ballad, and the one life
you get on earth tastes good. . . . What he doesn't
know yet is that, when he gets there and starts
asking, they'll tell him Jay's gone to Montana,
went to see a friend who lives on Flathead Lake,
without so much as goodbye or Please Forward.)

8.
1974

I'm with Walter now, he's driving, we've left
D.C. behind as we make our way northwest
through Maryland to Harper's Ferry — our first
road trip together, one of the scarce occasions
when we have time to go into our origins.
In shards and fragments, he gives the story
of his ancestors, gentlemen farmers in Hungary,
the War, the betrayals, the grandfather who
didn't survive Auschwitz;
the grandmother who did, her life as a cook
in Catskill resort hotels, lately retired
at a group home in Detroit. His own mother's death.
Silence and a hand placed lightly on his
are as much as I can do. Trees rushing by,
a sinking sun caught in them. Wordlessness,
more than anything else, was how we communicated.

Five o'clock when we arrive, but there's time
to stand on a bluff overlooking the handsome
confluence of the Potomac and Shenandoah,
several houses from the early 1800s
quietly regarding us while a twilight
soft as down creeps in from all sides,
scent of chestnut leaf and flower expanding,
a distant plash of waters, and the whispered
sensation of backward-stretching time, remote
and deep as Appalachia. A brief promenade's
muffled footfalls resound with the gravity
lent to any earth where blood was once shed.

On to Virginia, a hotel booked within sight

of the Blue Ridge. After dinner in our top-floor room
a windowseat offers the best prospect of the moon
levitating over black foothills, night breezes
heavy with perfume from flowers on the silk tree
below — a favorite species of Mr. Jefferson's,
I recall reading somewhere. From the pint flask
that used to go everywhere with me I've poured
a double shot these ice cubes will only halfway
cool down. Out over the lawn, fireflies bestir
themselves, rise, signal. An image floats up,
how five summers ago Ann and I caught them and turned
Mason jars into short-term, green-flickering lamps.
Would she remember that? I'll ask when we meet
next month. But wait, what was — ? A bright strobe
wide as the sky switches on, sheet-lightning playing
back and forth to the roll of monumental drums, and then
bang, another crackling flashbulb, the air charged
with electric prickles. Walter comes over, lounges
next to me and shares the light show. When
I turn, there's that serious-edged smile of his,
solemn eyes that seem to see everything. To break
the silence I ask, "Ever hear that old song, *Oh,
Shenandoah?*" I sing a few notes, a few wordless notes.

A few more, as we veered among the shifting vistas
of Skyline Drive in bright morning sunlight,
Milky Ways of wild daisies waving from roadside,
white and gold dots against windblown grasses.
Most worries seemed trivial up there on the blue
rooftop of Virginia, the "mother of presidents."
Conversation turned to poetry, that year's
paramount topic since things I'd written were now
appearing in print, the hoped-for endorsement
at last conferred. I didn't grasp how rare

his *a priori* support of the fantastic
project was, while I soldiered on without much
worrying about income, seconded by him,
an architect in the line of Wright and Kahn.
When we came down from the Blue Ridge, it was only
to push on to Charlottesville, the university
and another celebrated hill outside town, site
of our most versatile president's house.
The estate implied to some of its visitors
that those ideal, white-elephant fantasies
Americans have always had a weakness for at times
come true as shrine of beauty or cradle of thought
that then sets forth to revise the status quo.
Guided change, I mean, since nothing,
in any case, ever says the same. Even us.
We had two more years until dividing forces
clearer to me now than they were then sent him
elsewhere. But a quality of wordlessness
is still within reach, present in the snapshot
before me right now, and still emitting energy.
Hands on hips he smiles, standing beneath
frozen hands of the clock set over the door
of the domed house that has become the house we share.

(Henry Barstow in a field outside Front Royal
watches his son Billy tote the .22 he gave him
for his birthday. Safety's on, but the boy isn't
easy with it, clearly. He's just ten, an only child.
Henry's own twelve-gauge is like an extra trusty limb.
A little target practice and the boy'll feel handier
with his rifle. Morning sunlight flickering with wind
in the distant hickories. Billy stops and stoops down
to see something. "Look, Daddy, a butterfly."
Swallowtail flits up in the light, the boy smiles

at him. "It was drinking this pink flower." Nods
and says, "Let's keep moving, we've got a ways to go."
Yes, there's no better land anywhere. Henry plans
to turn over the farm to his boy one day, but maybe
Billy ought not to farm, no money in it. Hateful
what the world's become, lot of crooks running things.
If he sells up they'll just turn his farm into
a development. But what if he was forced to? Why,
Granddaddy'd climb out of his grave and knock him
cockeyed. Six generations on this farm. Well,
he probably won't have to. A redtail hawk floats
overhead. There. A likely stump to shoot at —
but where's Billy? Oh. Running up and holding out
a little bunch of wildflowers. "Here, Daddy, I picked
these for you." Billy's face changes when he stares
at him. "We don't have time for those, Son." Boy bites
his lip, looks down at the flowers. Henry has to choke
back the temptation to get mad, knows he shouldn't,
but, God, he doesn't want his son to turn out like that.
Life is hard enough and he cares for this boy more
than he knows how to say. "Here, Son, let's get some
practice with your gun." Bends down and takes it,
squats behind the boy. "Hold it like this." Stiffly.
"See that stump?" No answer. Then Billy turns around:
"Daddy? I'm scared." Their eyes lock. Who is more afraid?
In deep distance, a short blast from a train whistle,
the rush of eastbound wheels on steel, a gleam of light
across the miles; and the gritty taste of disappointment.)

9.
1989

Misgivings this December dusk are one mood
with falling snow that wipers left to right and back

brush off the windshield in crystal wedges,
things coming clear, then going dim again as I
try for some perspective. After the breakup
I'd planned at least two years of singlehood,
but here I am, caught off guard, launching out again,
even though we're both still in shock, even
though we live in different states, and my stint
in Cincinnati over with. Along the highway,
near a turnoff to Chillicothe, an old farm
swims into view, barn and house and one bare elm
reading as an oblique lithograph, endurance
in fine degrees of white and gray and solitude.
(Odd how that attic window's the only one lighted.)
When and where will I see you again? We'll write,
of course, a cool replacement for the kiss
still tingling on my ear, oh, *not* the last — .
The two hours to Columbus don't seem daunting
yet, and once there I can decide to stop
or go on. . . . (It turns out simple persistence and
the steady metronomic clearance of the windshield
suffice to get my blue Colt far as Akron
before it turns into a lit-up Holiday Inn.)

By morning strong sun is out and snow melting.
Today's offbeat itinerary: a wary drive
through Kent State to see where law and order
was once, no matter how, enforced; and Hiram College,
alma mater of a friend who'd been a life-raft
during the stormy year just past. Small town
Midwestern virtues are what I see in Hiram's
red brick, foursquare layout, its blending in
with the houses of the citizens — a public
peace and reliability that to New Yorkers
can only seem exotic as . . . as a cornfield. From there

to Garrettsville, Hart Crane's birthplace nine decades
earlier, though no bronze plaque anywhere tells
which weathered old gingerbread Gothic fantasy
belonged to Mr. Crane and his young bride. That one,
I arbitrarily decide and pay respects,
before continuing on to I-80 at Youngstown.
Hour by hour in the back of my mind you hover,
up and down over the Alleghenies, a glaze
of light on stands of evergreen, or the hush
that holds motionless flotillas of cloud high
above in a blue that seems to promise everything
without precisely spelling out what everything might be.

(Walker Tuggs steps down stiffly into the sunlight,
the door of the trailer slowly drifting shut.
He locks it. His trick knee hurts but he has to get
some groceries in. Drives to the Oak Mall.
A new check-out girl stares a bit, he being
one of the few colored in Columbiana County.
Nobody 72 with eyes can be surprised at that,
and by now it sure doesn't trouble him. Stare
right back. He's from Cincinnati, his people
go back to Kentucky and the underground railroad
but he prefers northern Ohio. Daughter still down there,
takes tickets at the Harriet Beecher Stowe House,
not ever going to marry. She keeps his paintings
in her back parlor, not a scrap of extra room here.
Years since anybody lifted a hand to sell them.
He unloads the Voyager, takes the stuff inside.
Not too many trailers installed in this park
and it's next to a nice stretch of woodland.
He might get back to painting some time.
Why, since he's been totally forgotten?
Well now. It could have gone different. He puts

the cans of Heinz beans on the shelf, the ribs
and six-pack in the fridge. In the late '30s,
they grouped him with protest painting just because
his subject was "the soul of black folk."
A few critics took interest, and then collectors.
Somewhere in the Museum of Modern Art's storage,
an early Walker Tuggs is a-moldering in its grave. . . .
After the war, he went back to work and *better* work,
but the scene had changed. And so had Harlem.
Things weren't so friendly, besides, deep down,
what we had was an Ohio boy, strictly cornbread
and collard greens, champagne didn't do that much
for him, and abstraction, why, next to nothing.
Abstract is just the skeleton you start with,
you got to put meat on the bones. Sure, he did
a couple of shows, but they didn't rock the rafters.
And he wasted a lot of time on a no-good broad,
and a lot of money at the races, ain't blaming
nobody. Seems like he always had a way of saying
the wrong thing, arrogant s.o.b. that he was.
And because he attended a few Party meetings,
word went out "Tuggs is a Commie," which was a lie,
he'd just gone to hear Paul Robeson speak.
Oh yes, a lot of people let him know one way
or another they were on his side, but handshakes
behind the scenes don't pay the rent, do they?
Most folks don't have a notion about what's good
anyhow till somebody with guts says real loud
which horse to pick, and then they trample each
other trying to bet on it. A gas, except if
you're not the favorite. Finally he got fed up,
came back to Cincy, drove a truck for P & G,
painted houses, married, lived in Over-the-Rhine,
and sometimes, of a Sunday afternoon, set up the easel.

Little Marlene would run up and grab his pants leg
and bother him, or Bertis would say fix the broken
lamp, so he didn't finish, why, three canvases a year.
Mr. Tyrone, his old teacher, died, about the last person
who was interested anyhow, and one day, blam, he
pitched the oil paints into the trash and went
on a three-day tear. Hasn't painted a lick since.
After Bertis died, he moved up to Youngstown,
lived with a gal who worked in a beauty salon
and sang weekends at the Flying Eagle Tavern.
He remembers one time Dakota Staton dropped by,
eventually gave in and did a song with the band.
Nice lady. Wasn't too long after that Jonelle
got on dope and in a month or two was good
for nothing, so he eased on out. He'll still go
into Youngstown now and then, whenever, you know,
the mood strikes to hear a little jazz music.
Columbiana has its share of two-bit rednecks,
but mostly they don't bother you if you don't them.
He sits down on the bed, reaches for the racing form,
by accident pushing *The Vindicator*
and a book of Romare Bearden's art to the floor.
Picks it up and looks at a few pictures,
goes back to the magazine. *Damn,* left the tap
dripping. Groans as he gets up, damn arthritis
in his knee. Sound of a car outside. Hold it,
what's that? Somebody knocking. He goes
first to the window. White fellow, sport jacket,
no tie, carrying a briefcase. Opens: "Yes?"
"Mr. Walker Tuggs?" "What do you want?"
Guy smiles. "The painter, Walker Tuggs?"
"I am. What can I do for you." Smiles again:
"Whew, did I have trouble finding you. May I come in?")

13.
1989

Last week of the year and there's a pall
of cloud over East Texas, roughly the same
color as the parched stretch of desert
dotted with sage the interstate divides,
a bone-white ribbon receding steadily west.
Thoughts come back from the trek through
nearly two years ago, when Sandy and I turned
onto state 71 just past Columbus, to make
a detour to Austin. The same cloud cover
that day also. Ladybird Johnson's policy
of public "beautification" had taken the form
of sowing wildflowers in colorful masses
along the highway shoulders — native lupine,
poppy, and daisies, mile after speeding mile.
Suddenly a flashing light: rats, the state patrol.
Forgot we'd left behind laissez-faire I-10.
It was pointless to argue. Ticket accepted,
we drove on to see our friends in Austin,
who sympathized with stories of their own
and took us to limestone cliffs above the river
for views of the old capital, identified
at dusk when a lone star rose and branded
the blue evening with its silver light.

That was then. This time I've taken I-20
to have a look at Dallas and Fort Worth (among
other attractions, the Kimbell Museum,
Louis Kahn's not yet surpassed temple of art).
A low-level disquiet buzzes through daydreams
as Nashville artists on the radio keep advising,
"All you need in life is one good well,"

or, "Love helps those who cannot help themselves."
And then the engine slings a rod and ratchets
nastily to a halt in the middle of nowhere.
Don't ever try to flag down cars with cruise
control set at 80 along straightaways in Texas.
Deep gratitude to Leroy Byrom of Des Moines
for giving me a lift into Dallas. He'd been
to see his folks in Little Rock and, as we drove,
played gospel songs composed and sung by him
an Albuquerque entrepreneur had promised
to do something with. His creamed-coffee hand
shook mine goodbye when he dropped me off
at a Howard Johnson's near the first exit
to Dallas. "Have a good life," I was urged
and have actually attempted to manage,
the first step a telephone call to triple-A,
who sent rescue in the form of a Ford tow truck.

(Victor Lopez of Arlington takes down
the genealogy he's been working on several years,
ever since he decided to find out about his roots.
The first part was easy, given his family
had records of the original grant on the Brazos
River, in what was called the Nile Valley   .
because of floods that struck from time to time
and redesigned the basin. Weren't many Jews
in Texas then, they didn't have a rabbi,
but observed as best they could. Before that
there were Lopez in Mexico and had been
since around 1650, emigrants from Brazil.
They'd come to Rio from southern France,
where the family had been living since Spain
kicked out everyone who wasn't Catholic.
First mention is of Arie ben Jacob of Toledo,

a metalsmith, whose son went to Avignon
after the expulsion and used the name Louppes.

The sound of a firetruck outside blares, subsides.
Victor makes some notes about other branches
of the family and then the telephone rings.
His wife Sharon, her voice tentative, whispery.
Nothing in particular, just wanted to talk.
"Look, I was thinking maybe a visit with Mother
tonight, OK? Want to come?" He agrees, hangs up.
She hasn't been well. At first they looked into
Epstein-Barr virus but finally decided
it was just depression. Began with her losing
her job at Houston and Klein Attorneys. People
being laid off because of the sluggish economy.
His gallery of Mexican antiques was doing poorly,
too, so no funds this year for private school,
which upset her because it was like starting out
with a handicap, and she hated that for the kids.
He promised to tutor them; but admitted the problem
was more complex. What can you do? But this will end,
and there's enough to see them through, just have
to wait it out. He had started going to Torah
study after temple on Saturdays, but Sharon wouldn't,
said that wasn't her family tradition. Victor
wishes she had something to get her out of herself.
He can't do much. The doctor's going to try Elavil.
Hope it's the right thing. Sam and Becky have been
kind of clingy lately, as though they'd regressed
a few years. he has to talk to them a lot,
what with Sharon staying in her room so they
won't see her crying. he thinks briefly of his
father's death, the kaddish, and sitting shiva.
Death is the only thing you don't have a chance

for a comeback. One day you're not. It's like a plank
that the person ahead of you walks — him first,
then it's your turn. Meanwhile you have your work,
and your family, things you care about. A few words
from kaddish float into his mind. The gold letters
on the spines of the books over his desk
glow in the afternoon light. *Blessed be He.* . . .
Been thinking of a ski trip to Steamboat Springs,
the kids, too, they say they want to learn. Sometimes
it's better to *pretend* things are going great,
then, like magic, they are. It's for Sharon.
A change of scene, a change of luck. The Rockies —
fantastic. Aspen's where they had their honeymoon.)

14.
1990

Palm trees along Santa Monica Boulevard,
puffs of domed cloud over the sea
and sleek Art Deco buildings
in the chalk-white light of March
set me adrift in a self-directed road movie
as I glided and wove among (Côte d'Azur
of the mind) the pastel sports cars, then turned
into a parking lot beside the theater.
A recently released *Henry V* —
the same director-actor whose *Midsummer
Night's Dream* was playing at the Taper Forum —
was what I'd come up with as a way
to fend off anxiously replayed projections
of your arrival here tomorrow. Would we
still feel as we did three months ago?
Be calm; enjoy the film. (Its freshest scene,
the young king's courtship of his lady — broken

music of her modest franglais and his
regal, boyish "maker of manners" dismissal
of French constraint in favor of a kiss.)

WELCOME TO LOS ANGELES says the sign, and here
by the freeway the red-lettered name of the concrete
construction company repairing embrasures
on an overpass is CAST OF THOUSANDS. The smile
that breaks across your bearded face when I point
toward it's worth these anxious weeks of waiting.
A cast of thousands's what in fact we have,
thousands of thousands here in this sneak preview
21st century on the Pacific Rim.
The Carnation sign looming over La Brea
if divided into two words sums it up
as the headless, tailless millipede
of cars, vans, and trucks creeps up 405
or down El Camino Real, my blue Colt
a single frame in a round-the-clock feature
that unpredictably jams but then resumes,
in a rhythm accepted by the stoic habitué,
each at last carried miraculously home.
A cast of thousands — but in this little
sublet house near the canals of Venice,
with palms, and poinsettias bright red even
now in the vigilant porch light, we are
only two, the door closed on everything
but the music, the candle, a dozen
carnations bought on last-minute impulse
that afternoon along with a sack of navel oranges
from a Chicano kid who, hesitant, trustful,
made the exchange from a traffic island on Fairfax.
Local wisdom says once you've merged top speed
onto I-10, rocketing west into the red ball

of six o'clock sun, "There's no turning back now."
One by one, defenses fall away, not strong enough
to cap the burning well, intensities I had
forgotten or no longer felt entitled to.

And when, two weeks later, we say goodbye,
What then? "If it's meant to continue, we'll
find a way." We will. Differences between us
are, possibly, what is most promising. A year's
wait, or more, we can manage if required to.
The royal palms stir and gesture agreement;
cloud terraces poise over the sea and put down
Feelers of light on molten waves where closer in
silhouettes of surfers crouch and zigzag forward
as a jet overhead wheels into its eastbound track.

(Kimberley Sternberg closes the door behind her
softly since Kevin has fallen asleep at last.
She left a note: "Dear Mr. Shanahan, Sleep well.
Your secret admirer returns tomorrow. Be ready."
The jeep backs out onto Spaulding, drops into first.
A deep breath. Feels great to have a night out.
Since Kevin was diagnosed a year ago, it's been
rocky. A lot of hours every day go to help out —
but if you're not there for your best friend,
what are you? "I hate AIDS," she sighs and sets
her jaw, lets herself wonder how long he's got and
how long before she has to find a new roommate.
Receptionists aren't paid all that well,
and rent in West Hollywood just keeps inflating.
Kevin gave up his work doing continuity for
Warner, just stays home and watches soaps all day.
He decided against any more injections for the lesions,
just too painful, don't let anybody tell you

interferon feels good when it goes under your skin.
He'd planned to go to Maui for a few days, then the guy
who'd invited him canceled for no real reason.
Kevin's been pleading with her for weeks to go out
and have fun, so when Todd telephoned from Sedona,
she said, sure, they could meet, love to. You have
to be flexible with Todd, he's always on location,
you never know when he'll call. In love with him?
Yes. No. Since there's no real possibility.
She's getting tired, though, of hearing Tanya's
soundbites about what a mistake getting involved
with married guys is. People do what they have to do.
Wouldn't you know the nail on her middle finger'd
break this morning when she was trying to unscrew
the lid of a jar of buckwheat honey. Oh well.

She turns onto Sunset, and wonders why Todd always
has to stay at the Beverly Hills, invariably
in one of the bungalows out back. Advantage is,
she knows the drill: you park in that little street
behind the hotel, follow a path between palm trees
and shrubbery right up to the swimming pool
and the bungalows. That way you skip the front desk
so nobody has to know that Todd's seeing someone
and maybe tell Renée, not to mention the tabloids.
How *do* those guys put up with being trailed
by flashbulbs everywhere they go? Oh, a full moon,
how mushy. She remembers the last time she was here
a hooker was doing exactly the same thing — like, what
else could the girl have been, in that leather getup? —
and they kind of smiled at each other, which made
her feel weird. Yes, but when Todd opened the door,
she stepped into his arms and pretended to be that girl . . .
and so when they came up for air, Todd said, "Hey,

that wasn't a kiss, that was a breathalyzer."
And on from there. She looks in the rearview mirror,
turns her head from side to side, puts on more lipstick
and blots it, the duller red imprint on the Kleenex
symmetrical, parted, split with white. Wads it up,
steps out, locks the car, and then sees the silhouette
of a big guy standing there staring at her, not moving.
Oh, a cop. "See your driver's licence, please?")

15.
1971

Coming back at the end of our last Northwest summer,
Ann and I decided to take the ferry across
Lake Michigan. A night in Escanaba,
which turned out to be something of a resort.
We noticed a weathered beauty queen — blonde,
wearing a white suit and seagreen blouse,
Chanel bag swinging from long gold chain —
walk unsteadily into the Escanaba Hotel
with her partner (in a dark blazer, also tipsy).
Cocktail piano tinkled "Stardust" and "As Time
Goes By" through the foyer, a stylishly
maritime atmosphere from the lake underscored
by bits of netting on the walls, shells, wheels,
cork floats. After dinner, up in our room, an hour
or two to sort through snapshots from the last
few months, who would keep which, and why. Somber
courtesy had governed every word and deed
all summer. Was it imaginative concern
anticipating the moment when we'd send
each other separate ways with a wan smile
and parental pat on the shoulder? Meanwhile
here were the pictures, what, of sky-blue gentians

and scarlet monkeyflowers in a grassy meadow
near Logan Pass high up in Glacier Park.
Or trembling aspens by a run of white water.
Or the Pacific, seen from Mount Neahkahnie.
Oh, somehow to keep what has been lived, this
perishable choreography of our pathfinding
through the years. . . . I paused over a shot
of the South Dakota Badlands, burnt lunar rocks
where nothing grew, the only sound a hidden chitter
of desert crickets. Now, even two months after,
shimmering heatwaves boiled up and scorched my hand.
Next day, our car in the hold, we stood on deck
to watch the churning wake dissipate farther
and farther behind into the orange track of the sun.
A blast from the stack seemed to echo that other
steamship passage a short four years ago
when we'd boarded a liner bound for France.
A briefer trek, this one, not a crossing
to the Old World. It was, in fact, the home
stretch, endowed with whatever advantages
accrue to realism, so that without forcing
I could see intelligence and experience
at my side, sunlight caught in stray wisps
of hair, and even a touch of indulgence
in the half smile and arched eyebrow
that seemed to ask, "What are you looking at?"

(In Traverse City Mary Mankaja, 19,
plunges up to her elbows in the soapy water
back in the kitchen of the Lake Cafe.
She's only been doing this a week and figures
maybe two more to save enough for a ticket
back to the Canyon. When she gets to Peach Springs,
she'll telephone and somebody will bring horses

up to Hualapai Hilltop to get her. She sees
the whole trip down, back and forth on the
switchbacks until they get to the Canyon floor.
Then the twin columns of Wigleeva Rocks,
and there will be the Creek and she'll
be home. She throws a pot into the rinse sink.
This didn't turn out, but she'll get back.
Tourists have been coming to Havasupai
since she was as big as a gopher, and why
this time did she get involved? Because Fernando
had studied — what was it, you know, tribes
and their cultures. He was Chicano, born
in Las Cruces. Had gone to college, but was
different from Anglos, not stupid. So when
he asked her to come with him, she thought about it.
She'd been outside to school but never far away.
He said she ought to see things at least. There's not
that much to do in the Canyon, except cooking
and laundry and swimming at the Falls, and an old
movie once a week at the Recreation Center
about whites against Indians. Nobody in Supai
has any money to travel. So she said yes.
Didn't come home from the trip up to the Rim,
just telephoned and told them she was leaving.
Mother said, "We'll be here." It was fun at first.
They went to Phoenix and ate in restaurants.
In the motel room he would tell her to stand
in the middle of the bed and hold her hair up
over her head and he would just look. It felt
as though she had flown up into the stars
next to the moon and could stay if she wanted to.
But meanwhile there was the table next to the bed,
with a lamp and an ashtray and a bottle of lotion.
Through the window she could see his white Dart

in the parking lot. So she was still on earth.
He took her to dance bars, but she was too shy.
A lot of it scared her. When waitresses would ask,
"Where are y'all from?" she didn't want to say.
One night he got drunk and told her he had a wife.
He hadn't seen her for a long time and didn't think
they could get back together. He admitted being
confused and said it was from trying to live
in two different worlds. He didn't know what
he was going to do when his money ran out.
It went down from there. He wasn't the only thing
she didn't understand. It was embarrassing.
She had to explain that growing up in the Canyon
in a way had been very protective, a lot
on the outside seemed stupid and you missed
having your people around you, even though sometimes
they were boring. She misses them now and wishes
she were walking down the main street, her feet
in the warm dust, the cottonwoods giving shade,
the green smell of their leaves in the air,
the shadow of a horse moving across the ground. . . .
Anyway, one night they drove into Traverse City
and found a motel, and he got real serious. He said
it was time for them to split up, he had to go
back home. She cried. He spoke soft to her and held her,
but her heart had turned into a rock. She got up,
told him to give her twenty dollars, which he did,
and she walked out, just like that. When she has
that feeling of being on the right track, she never
worries, she knows it will come out in a good way.
Maybe it was good she got a chance to see it all.
She'll be back in time for Peach Festival,
the kids will be going away to school, she'll tell
them a couple of things to watch out for, and life

will turn back to the way it's always been.
She doesn't care if she never gets married, either,
as long as the water of the Havasu is green and cool.)

19.
1989

I'd started out in Saratoga Springs
and taken I-90 west, through the Finger Lakes,
Seneca Falls, all the way to Buffalo.
On Enola Ave., in the ghetto, a shirtless boy,
eight or nine, held up a placard that said,
"Car wash $.30," and an Exxon attendant
gave me directions for Art Park (that encounter
of American sculpture with open American air).
The viewing platform over the plunging river
put the idea in my head to revisit the Falls,
which Ann and I had seen from Canada just twenty
years ago. So, after finding a motel on Grand Island
and having my dinner, I drove up to see it.
All changed. Spotlights kept the torrent visible
while amplifiers from the mall galvanized
the night with Handel's "Water Music," a neon
light-show synesthetically echoing each
counterpointed voice. Now for a broad, slow rainbow
projected across the cataract so good taste
might be once again defeated utterly.
Crowds upon crowds of viewers laughing,
talking — Latino, Japanese-, English-, Polish-American —
thrilled to be there with the children
for this popular epiphany freely espoused
in the land of liberty. How free was I?
Free enough to forgo a reflex groan and to
allow that human happiness is various,

that no one has everything — nor could I in all
solemnity have taken them along earlier
in the day to gaze at a ziggurat of rusted
oildrums titled "Drums Along the Niagara,"
to mention only one work in the exhibition.

Morning. Mild sunlight along Lake Erie,
a Mediterranean shore with vineyards
and red-tiled roofs that bespeak Italy
as much as the Great Lakes. I'm on my way
to Indiana, hope to make Columbus, OH,
by nightfall. Overlapping geographies
unpack their stories: one about returning
East more than a year ago on I-70,
a pause to have a look at Martin's Ferry,
where Roebling's first suspension bridge connects
the town to Wheeling, WV. Plainspoken names,
unmemorialized outside the aggrieved
dreamwork of James Wright — who also found
a latter-day beatitude among the vineyards
and pines of Tuscany before he came back home
to die.
        Telescoped time-frames: could I foresee,
as I circled Ohio's capital city that night,
I'd be living there the following year,
you coming up from Cincinnati every weekend
to survey the world together from our top floor
on Jefferson Avenue? Or set off again on joint
excursions — to Chicago, for the Lyric Opera,
or Columbus (the Indiana one), where classic
modern buildings commissioned the past
five decades form an ideal urban habitat.
From now forward these interstates will read
as a palimpsest, a layered narrative

for the portable home entertainment center
consciousness is, the fluent, interior
Niagara. . . .
               It rains, the sun rises and sets
on the just and the unjust. Two days more, and here
was New Harmony, down in the southwest corner
of Indiana, on the banks of the Wabash, a grid
of streets lined with golden raintrees brought
from Mexico during the last century. Half
a month in a restored house, with no duties
except daily self-assigned hours at the desk.
Notes for "La Madeleine." A translation project.

But not all day. One afternoon I drove to see
Angel Mound State Park, site of an ancient town
built by the Middle Mississippian Culture
and abandoned during the fourteen hundreds.
Furnace heat, shrilling cicadas, sluggish river.
A line of oaks in the distance, high Temple Mound
with reconstructed sanctuary, windowless.
Inside, glints of light slipped through the thatching.
A baked clay basin for fires. Presence of the dead.
The sense of being watched, my thinking overheard,
sifted, to know which blessing ought to be conferred.

And back in town, having made some headway, there
was time to have a meal at the house of the last
descendant bearing the surname of Robert Owen —
who wore his eighty-six years serenely, pleased
to talk about Kentucky horses, the Saratoga
track, and the way things went before the war.

(Al Carson, 46, of Indianapolis
has come down with his wife to spend a few days

with her sister. He can take off any old time now,
since he's been on disability for a year.
Before, he worked in a die-cast factory
for automobile parts. The robots in the electric-
hydraulic system broke, spilled some oil
that caught fire. He and the others got out,
but not before they breathed enough smoke
to choke a horse. When the foreman told him,
Report for work tomorrow, the plant would be
operating again, they almost went knuckle junction,
except he was too weak. Not well yet, and will he
ever be? His wife Barbara got part-time work
at a day-care center, to help make ends meet.
At least the kids are grown. Bobby Jo works
at the Southroads Mall out in Tulsa,
and Al Jr. has gone to help his granddad,
who runs a service station in Willow Springs,
Missouri. He's a boy likes country ways,
and it's true there's no more beautiful land
than the Ozarks. Al wishes he could go back,
but Barbara has family, friends and church
in Indianapolis, she's president of her
Eastern Star chapter, and says, Let's please stay,
she never specially cared for the Show Me State.
No, and Al's not too crazy about her sister Myra,
either, but this old house of hers has lots of room,
and it makes a change to come down. Nothing much
to do, of course. He went with them yesterday
to buy groceries, said he'd get some bananas.
But it's hard to find any that aren't either
green or rotten nowadays. As he was picking
through them, Myra came up and said, "Come on, Al,
you're not buying a Cadillac," which she thought
was real cute. He got even later on, though.

When she washed her hair and put it in curlers,
he pointed and asked, "What channels do you get?"
"More than you do," is all she said. Man don't work,
women don't respect him, simple as that. He just
can't get his strength back. Doesn't even want
to go to the 500 any more. Doctor says,
Be patient, and that's what he is, a patient. Damn
hot today. He goes to the screen door and looks out
in the back yard, where Barbara aims the garden
hose on her nephew Harold, stampeding around
in a green swimsuit and yelling like an Apache.
On impulse, Al steps out on the porch and down
to the lawn, takes the hose from Barbara, who says
"What on earth," as he douses his head with water. . . .
She smiles, wipes his forehead, just like the good old days.
Hands the boy the hose and laughs, "Let's go inside, Al.")

20.
1992

Dolores and Wayne Davis have retired and are living in a condo
in St. Croix. Their son Herbert manages the citrus groves from an
office in Tampa. This October afternoon, their grandson knocks
on a door in Ybor City, pays, gets his bag, returns to the car, drives
to his girlfriend's apartment. She says she bleached the works
while he was gone, so they are ready to use. His father picks up
the phone and dials

Mike Kovich has been managing a hardware store in The Dalles
for ten years. He has remarried and has one son. His daughter
Amber visited in August and has gone back to her husband in
Wichita. Connie married a highway contractor years ago and is
doing volunteer work for elementary school literacy in Salt Lake.
Mike wonders whether

Billy Barstow has his own architectural firm in Baltimore. He lives with an English professor at Johns Hopkins. Henry Barstow had them visit at the farm in the Valley, but hasn't been willing to come to them in Baltimore. He has had to sell off a few acres of bottom land to keep the place. Lately, he's been experimenting with a new

Walker Tuggs had his first retrospective at the Carnegie-Mellon Gallery in Pittsburgh, a catalogue and monograph printed to go with it. He has no plans to move from Columbiana, but he is painting again. The thing about landscape is

Victor Lopez is on a business trip to Morelia in Mexico. His wife Sharon is doing well, with a job in development at the Kimbell Museum. Becky has one more year at school and Sam is in his first term at Kenyon. It's a brilliant day, with blue skies and a few racing clouds moving east. Sharon notices

Kevin Shanahan died of lung congestion brought on by Kaposi's sarcoma last summer. Kimberley Sternberg has moved to a smaller apartment in Los Feliz. She's biding her time while Todd's divorce gets worked out. Meanwhile he pulled strings and got her work as assistant to a casting director at Paramount, which she likes a lot. She misses Kevin, and is planning to go to Honolulu with one of his friends as soon as she

Mary Mankaja was thrown from a horse last month and broke her leg. She's mending and her son is helping with the chores. She almost never leaves Supai any more. But her husband Peter does, since he's been appointed to deal with the State Government. It wasn't the horse's fault, its hoof slipped on a rock in the creek and she was thrown. Next year

Al Carson's health has improved and he is doing house-painting in Indianapolis. His wife was kept on at the day-care center and has returned from a visit with her daughter in Tulsa. Her nephew Harold worked as a lifeguard this summer at the pool in Harmonie State Park. He's good at basketball and

You came to New York in January of last year, and you plan to stay, for better or for worse, richer, poorer, in sickness and in health. The day begins with you, ends with you. This first year of bereavement in the aftermath of my father's death. Late summer sees us take a long walk down from Columbus Circle all the way to Washington Square, and, look, the fountain sends up a high, foaming pillar of water. . . . Your thirty-fifth birthday falls in mid-October, and what we're going to do

Title and First Line Index